SONS OF ZULU

by the same author
THE MAGIC WORLD OF THE XHOSA

SONS OF ZULU

AUBREY ELLIOTT
with photographs by the author

COLLINS
London · Johannesburg
1978

William Collins Sons and Co Ltd
London · Glasgow · Johannesburg
Sydney · Auckland · Toronto

First published 1978
© Aubrey Elliott 1978

ISBN 0 00 216785 9

Produced in the Republic of South Africa
Typesetting in Plantin by McManus Bros.
Reproductions by Hirt & Carter
Printed and bound by ABC Press (Pty.) Ltd.

TO BILLY

Sir William Collins loved this land
and all that nature gave it and in
his enthusiasm insisted that I write
this book about one of its peoples

Contents

Acknowledgements

In the years it took me to complete the *Sons of Zulu* I had many interesting and exciting experiences during my research journeys in the field and when photographing the people in their traditional environment. Among the personal memories which I cherish are those of the scores of Zulu men, women and children and of the many white people of Natal and KwaZulu, and elsewhere in South Africa, who never tired of helping me, each in their own way.

The enthusiasm of those who became involved with my activities and were drawn into my task made me realise how many people there are, black and white, who are just as anxious as I am to conserve the knowledge of the culture and way of life of the Zulu traditionalists. The help of these people was unstinted and of inestimable worth to me and I thank them all most sincerely for their co-operation and assistance.

Their names are listed alphabetically:

Bantu Administration Department (now Department of Plural Relations) – their officials in many areas were always helpful and co-operative and assisted me in countless ways.

Dr. Peter Becker – in our association his tremendous interest in and knowledge of the Zulu not only inspired me in my own work, but out of our chats new ideas were born in my mind.

Mr. C. T. Binns – a dear friend and a man of many parts including that of historian of the Zulu and a student of their culture. In his affectionate warmth and endless generosity, he shared his extensive knowledge with me. He has since 'gone back Home' – as the Zulu would say – to join the ranks of his Ancestors.

Mr. Bradley – ethnologist of Nongoma. His on-the-spot information was particularly valuable.

Mr. George Bunting – one of the greatest living authorities on the Battles of Isandlwana and Rork's Drift and a fascinating *raconteur*.

Mr. P. W. Boshoff – at that time an official of the Department of Bantu Administration in Nkandla. He took me on some remote routes which I would otherwise never have found.

The Killie Campbell Africana Library – by allowing me to photograph their old paintings, they added a valuable and necessary facet to my book.

Mr. Induna Cele – an old Zulu man who individually gave me hours of his time and who never tired of telling me of his people's customs.

Mr. and Mrs. Hugh Comrie – they shared their home with me many times and with it much information on Zulu customs.

Mr. De Lange – Bantu Affairs Commissioner at Nkandla.

Mrs. Maura de Havilland – my editorial assistant. Her help was indispensable and without it the completion of this book would have taken very much longer than it did.

My wife, Irma – she not only contributed substantially to the production of this work by her patient understanding during the untold hours when I was glued to my desk, but in addition she patiently and meticulously typed and retyped the manuscript.

Dr. Rosalie Finlayson of the University of South Africa for her part in reading the manuscript and offering constructive criticism on various aspects of it.

'Oom' Arie Harris – discussions at his home on the banks of the White Mfolozi River yielded many treasures of information, gathered over the years of his life among the Zulu.

Mr. Kingsley Holgate and his wife, Jill, for their friendship and their hospitality which I enjoyed during my many visits to them and which I always remember. Without Kingsley's help my studies would have proved much less rewarding than they were.

Mr. A. D. McKay – his help during the early stages of my work on this book was particularly important and made my task a great deal easier.

Mr. F. J. Malan – once again as in *The Magic World of the Xhosa* proved to be a valuable source of information.

Mr. Ian Matthews – he generously shared his extensive knowledge of the customs and beliefs of the tribal Zulu with me.

Mr. Christian Msimang of the University of South Africa – he not only edited the Zulu words used in my text but also provided a fine incentive for me with his great enthusiasm for the need of this book about the traditions of the Zulu.

Miss Diana Newham – who at a time when I was hard-pressed to meet publishing deadlines, came to the rescue and provided valued editorial assistance.

The *Ngonyama* ('Lion'), King Zwelithini Goodwill KaCyprian Bhekuzulu – the courteous reception accorded me at his 'Great Place' I mention with special appreciation.

Mr. Hezekiel Ntuli who has since gone on to the Place of his Ancestors – a Zulu man of the kraals with extreme sensitivity and high intelligence. A sculptor in clay whose work is much sought after in Natal. He was also a natural historian among his people and told me many fascinating tales.

Mr. Otte, the magistrate at Nongoma – his vast knowledge of the Zulu and their ways brought to light some fascinating aspects of tribal culture.

Mr. Joe Pohl – the battlefield of Qokli Hill lies on his farm and with his co-operation I was able to make a detailed study of this area.

Mr. Martin Rudd for his artistic presentation of a Zulu kraal based on my rough sketches and descriptions.

Mr. Walter Sokela – in spite of the short period of our acquaintance, I was able to gather a vast amount of important information about Zulu culture from him. He lost his life tragically.

Mr. Graham Stewart – at an orthodox Zulu Kraal he has done much to preserve a vanishing culture and I owe him a debt of gratitude for his assistance particularly in the field of photographic subjects and models.

Mr. Corrie Stroebel – whilst he was in the Department of Tourism in Eshowe, his help was invaluable in introducing me to many sources of information and in his enthusiasm he himself gathered many facts which I might otherwise not have found.

Mr. Henry Torlage – Commissioner General of the Zulu National Unit. He introduced me to the *Ngonyama* at his "Great House", and, with his warm hospitality and co-operation, added a great deal of interest to my research.

Dr. Barbara Tyrrell – it would be difficult to express my appreciation adequately to this good friend and fellow-anthropologist. Our paths through a fascinating field of research have crossed many times and over the years she has shared a great deal of her deep knowledge of the customs of the tribal peoples with me.

The University of South Africa and in particular the Principal – Prof. T. van Wijk – and the Heads of the Departments of African Languages and of Anthropology, Professors J. A. Louw and A. C. Myburgh (now retired) respectively. Their sustained interest in my work was a continuous source of encouragement to me.

Mr. Rayno van Rooyen and his wife, Margaret – at their trading store I found a wealth of colourful material related to the local Cele Clan and at their home always a welcome.

My son Wayne and my daughter Margaret – they provided cheerful and welcome company on some of my field trips when they were able to accompany me.

Mr. Harold Wilmot – from his modern store in Nqutu, near the battlefield of Isandlwana, his help was invaluable in many ways.

Mrs. Beryl Wood – talented artist who not only depicts the tribespeople as subjects of her exquisite drawings, but also has a fine knowledge of their traditions. To her I express my sincere thanks for reading the manuscript and for offering me the benefit of her constructive suggestions.

In the final analysis I cannot but comment on the pleasure which I derived from the *photography* for this book. Much of it grew out of the light-hearted fun which the Zulu of the kraals had in being the centre of attraction – the echoes of their laughter still ring in my ears – and much of it was born out of the natural pleasure inherent in photography. For the most part I seldom carried less than three cameras which were almost invariably Mamiya. I loaded them with different film for specific purposes or conditions and then, in addition, kept spare ready-loaded film backs for quick renewal of film when the action was fast as in a dance sequence. By using interchangeable lenses I often got a picture which I might otherwise have missed because the subject was either too wide or too distant for a standard lens. So, remembering the excitement with which they provided me and the contribution which they made towards a preservation of something of Zulu history, I must in conclusion and in gratitude express my appreciation of my friends, my cameras.

AUBREY ELLIOTT
Pretoria
1978

Introduction

A century has passed since the warriors of old Zululand armed with their spears and their shields and unbelievable gallantry, earned for themselves a reputation which perhaps has few parallels of its type in the annals of history.

The epic of their adventures reads like a legend. It began, of course, in 1816 with the advent of a genius named Shaka Zulu but to the wide world abroad, the year which gave the Zulu their supreme crown of glory was 1879. On the 22nd January of that year, Zulu King Cetshwayo's warriors devastated Lord Chelmsford's forces at Isandlwana in an hour and a half in one of the worst defeats the British have ever known. The Zulu then went on to beleaguer the Redcoat garrison at Rorke's Drift only a few kilometres away and engaged them through the night in a battle so fierce that, in its twelve hours' duration, eleven British soldiers won the Victoria Cross for their gallantry – something never before equalled in British history.

The adventures of those barefooted warriors of old left such vivid impressions on the mirror of the world's mind that they still linger there today.

But what of their descendants? That is what this book is about.

Sons of Zulu is not about the nation in its entirety, but about the last of the old orthodox tribespeople living in remote parts of their homeland and who have not yet involved themselves in 'civilization' much beyond the nearest trader's store. These people still follow some of the customs evolved by their predecessors and they practice rites which come out of the mists of time from some unknown land far beyond South Africa's borders. Some of these practices are so far removed from today's world that they are unknown to and certainly not followed by the educated city brothers of the Kraal people.

The daily life of these tribal folk is still wrapped in myth and mystery. Witches bedevil their paths and witch-doctors – diviners – are their mentors and earthly refuge in times of fear.

They worship the spirits of their ancestors, who reward them with good fortune when they offer sacrifices and punish them when they do not. Nature herself was the architect who worked out for these people a pattern of life close to her bosom, with behavioural codes and laws evolving from the need to protect their society and to give it orderliness.

But the march of time is inexorable. The white man's way of life is an irresistible force and a powerful magnet and before long the last of the old culture, which I have been fortunate to find in the quiet hills and distant parts of Zulu country, will be lost forever and known no more to the new sons of Zulu. With these thoughts in mind, I traversed Natal and Zululand, or Kwazulu as it is known today, many times and in the pages of this book I have tried to recreate some of my impressions and to tell something of the character and characteristics of the country Zulu as I found them.

In my photographs I have set out to portray the gaiety, the friendliness and the good humour which I encountered everywhere in my travels.

Chapter 1
The First Zulu

The romance which surrounds the name of the Zulu nation has lingered on for a century or more since the days in the mid-eighteen hundreds when their exploits were blazoned in dramatic headlines across the world.

The tales of their deeds during those warring years read like legends of forgotten times, but the Zulu epic is no fantasy. Even though they have not been known as an established race for nearly as long as, for instance, the Xhosa they certainly experienced more excitement and drama in the few lively decades when they were engraving their name into the pages of history, than have any of Southern Africa's other black peoples.

So much has already been written about those eventful years that there is little need for me to return to them in any detail here, but I intend, nevertheless, to recapitulate a little of their historical background in order to illustrate how and to what extent it played a role in shaping the character of the Zulu man, woman and child of today.

Beyond that, this book is about the rural descendants of those old warriors – the men and women of the present generation who have continued to live in their valleys and on their hillsides in traditional kraals, or homes, very much in the way that their ancestors did. Despite a tendency among the younger generation to move into the cities and the white man's civilisation, these people have remained in their traditional rural environment.

They, these country Zulu, form the hard-core of the nation. Many of them still practise customs which are so old that they have no known origin and they believe in all manner of supernatural powers. For instance, the mystery of lightning often terrifies them with its potential consequences. They dabble in magic and medicine. Diviners – who are perhaps better known as witchdoctors – are their mentors.

Kwazulu defined Today the homeland of the Zulu in South Africa is comprised of areas stretching in the main from the Indian Ocean in the east to the Drakensberg mountains in the west and from the Pongola River in the north, to the Tugela in the south, with an overflow of additional areas located further south in Natal. There are, of course, also many Zulu who live in the Province of Natal itself, where they are employed in many different spheres in the country and in the towns.

The Zulu call their homeland KwaZulu, which in their own language means 'the place of the Zulu'. Literally, in English, this is simply Zululand.

In the early stages of this book I refer to the country before about 1819 as 'Nguniland' because, until then, it was not ruled by the Zulu nor was there even a Zulu *nation* as such, only a tiny *clan* by that name. The population of Nguniland at that stage, was made up of many isolated family groups and clans who were largely nomadic and went their own way, as and where they chose, in search of grazing for their cattle or of game. Their doctrine was: 'The land, like the rain, belongs to no-one. It is there for all to share'.

13

Today, the people of KwaZulu call themselves, collectively, 'amaZulu' which means 'the Zulu people'. The literal meaning of the word 'Zulu' is 'sky' or 'the blue space above'. It may also refer to 'heaven' in the Christian context, but, since the pagan tribesman has no equivalent of heaven – nor any of hell – I personally prefer to interpret 'Zulu' to mean the sky and 'amaZulu' to mean 'the people of the sky'.

This is, of course, always remembering that the people of the Zulu *clan*, which is itself part of the Zulu nation are, in another sense, additionally 'sons of Zulu' by being descendants of their progenitor by that name.

The Place of the Spirits

It is, perhaps, of interest to mention here that whenever I have asked Zulu people what they think the sky above actually is, they have invariably replied, with an indifferent wave of their hands, '*Hawu!* that's *nothing*, that just wind up there'.

Apparently they do not even consider the sky as a possible place where the spirits of their ancestors may dwell. On the contrary, they are more inclined to believe that the ancestral spirits have a place *inside* the earth which seems more logical to them because it is solid and firm. Others I have spoken to have even suggested that perhaps the spirits live upside down under the earth.

They have a lovely supporting theory for this idea, which they relate to dreams. The Zulu believe implicitly that dreams are the media through which their ancestors speak to them, but the people themselves can seldom interpret the messages contained in these dreams as they are so often 'opposite' in meaning. This is where their theory that spirits live under the earth gets support. They say that when it is night time on earth, and dark, and people are asleep and dreaming, then it is day time underneath and the spirits are about their affairs. That is when the spirits speak to their families on earth, but because it is light there and dark here, their messages come through in reverse, like for example when a black *cow* is seen in a dream it will in reality turn out to be a white *ox*.

It is largely because the ordinary people can seldom understand a dream, that they call in the diviners (witchdoctors) to interpret the message for them, because diviners are the intermediaries between earth-dwellers and their spiritual families.

Malandela the Progenitor

Historians have traced the beginnings of the Zulu clan back to about 1670 to an old black man who lived a nomadic life in the Babanango area of Natal's northern midlands. In his wanderings, he ultimately found a haven on the picturesque western slope of Mandawe Hill, 14 kilometres outside of Eshowe. He was Malandela, reputedly son of Luzumane. His wife was Nozinja ('mother of' or 'Ms. Dogs'), and they had at least two known sons, Qwabe and Zulu, and a small following of adherents.

Malandela's name, somewhat inappropriately, means 'the one who follows', but it is unlikely that it had any connection with leadership. It suggests, instead, that he was not the firstborn child of his father, but rather, 'the-one-who-followed-his-elder-brother'. Mandawe Hill is a majestic and beautiful place set in lush greenery and the hill so impressed old Malandela that he decided to settle there with his little band and roam no more. Today the main road from Eshowe to Melmoth passes within a few hundred metres of where his kraal must have stood in the morning shadow of the hill.

14

The tales of old kraals have it that Malandela* was not long spared to enjoy his hillside but he was, nevertheless, at a ripe old age when 'he went back home to join his ancestors'.

His eldest son and logical heir was Qwabe, but there was also Qwabe's brother *Zulu*. Legend has it that their mother, Nozinja, was a hard-working woman and not only supported them but began to gather together a small herd of white cattle. Qwabe, however, was not overattentive to his family and left them to go off on his own. Later, when he heard how the white herd had grown, he thought it would be a good idea to return home and gain his mother's favour once more. Nozinja, however, realised what his motives were and decided not to favour him to the detriment of her younger son, Zulu, who had stood by her through her hardest years.

Mpungose, the Loyal
Servant

Because of this, a rift then developed in the family and Nozinja broke up home and moved away to the north with Zulu, her herd, and a loyal manservant named Mpungose. They left the beautiful Mandawe Hill, crossed the hot Mhlatuze lowlands and ascended the hills beyond in the direction of Melmoth. They then went up the Mfule River valley to its source and settled a little beyond the hills of the White Mfolozi River, in a spot about 95 km inland from the Indian Ocean.

They were three people and a few white cattle.

Belonging to a patriarchal society as the little household did, Zulu, son of Malandela, became its head because a woman – in this case, his mother – is always subservient to the senior man in the home.

In due course, Zulu took a wife from a clan in the neighbourhood and his son or sons took the name Zulu as their *sibongo* or family name. In this way the Zulu clan had its beginnings and the flimsy foundation of a nation was laid.

Before I go further, I cannot resist telling here that the third member of the little trio, the humble but loyal Mpungose, grew in confidence and stature under his young patron and was eventually released from service – probably after Nozinja died – and built his own home. He governed it well and *his* household, too, grew and became what to this day is the Mpungose clan.

Zulu's elder brother Qwabe, for his part, gave his name to a large group of followers who today are one of the biggest clans in KwaZulu. Both clans pay ultimate allegiance to the Zulu king.

The Family Tree

History attributes little of importance to the life of Zulu apart from his contribution of a name of which most chieftains would be proud. And so it was too with the reigns of his successors, *Punga, Mageba, Ndaba, Jama* and *Senzangakona*. They left no signs of any great deeds in their own right as warriors, but Senzangakona left a great heritage to the Zulu people in an illegitimate son given him by Nandi, a girl of the Langeni clan. That boy was Shaka Zulu . . . born about 1787. He was a genius who in his brilliance was almost a freak of nature.

Chief Senzangakona fell into disrepute because of his illicit love affair with Nandi. He married her ultimately to satisfy the Zulu code of honour, but when Shaka was only six, he expelled both of them from his royal kraal after a quarrel. He left them to find a living as best they could. They suffered desperately.

*Dr. A. T. Bryant gives his era as c1597 to c1691.

Times of drought fell upon them and food became as hard to find as friends. The little boy and his mother wandered from temporary refuge to temporary refuge. As he grew, Shaka's humiliation grew with him. Then, to add to this, his masculinity was slow in developing, with the result that his playmates teased him incessantly. They victimised him, too, because he was an outcast 'prince'. Bitterness welled up in him and, with it, a burning desire for revenge on everyone who had hurt him and the mother whom he dearly loved. This desire to vindicate himself may be blamed for the violence which punctuated his actions in later life and his determination to prove his power to himself and to those around him.

The Zulu 'Chiefs' before Senzangakona were, in reality, nothing more than the heads of a growing family group, but by his time the family was justified in calling itself a clan – the Zulu clan.

Shaka as Heir

Even so, at Senzangakona's death, it still numbered only about seventeen hundred people and carried little weight. On the contrary, the Zulu were vassal to a strong neighbouring tribe called the *Mtetwa* and paid allegiance to their chief, Dingiswayo – a man who played an important role both directly and indirectly in the history of the Natal Nguni people. The Nguni are, of course, the basic ethnic group from which the people of KwaZulu originated.

Directly, Dingiswayo's influence was in his fine leadership of a combination of clans which he had welded together, and indirectly it was in the fact that he took the destitute young exile, Shaka, under his wing when the boy was in his teens and trained him as a soldier and a leader.

By 1816 Shaka had a tremendous reputation in Dingiswayo's army, not only as a fighting man with a broad-bladed assegai or spear which he had introduced, but as a clever strategist in battle and as a leader. By this time Shaka's father, Chief Senzangakona, was old and fading and Shaka was his eldest living son. Although not the undisputed heir, he regarded himself as a legitimate claimant to the Zulu chieftaincy.

By Zulu tradition the eldest son of the chief is not automatically the first in line of succession. The chief may, in his lifetime, publicly nominate his successor from among any of his sons, but if he does not, the position can be confused and explosive because the people have no powers of appointment. No-one can, of course, stop them from taking sides.

Senzangakona, in his latter days, unmistakably made it clear that he favoured a son named Sigujana – son of one of his wives named Bibi – but he apparently never formally nominated him as successor. Even if he had, however, it probably would have made no difference to the trend of events which followed.

After a long period of weakening, old Senzangakona quietly 'went back home'. This is a lovely phrase the Zulu use to announce a man's passing. It is made the more poignant by their real belief that he returns to his Creator who then ultimately initiates him into the ranks of his family's ancestors.

By Zulu tradition, when a chief dies, it is given out that he is 'indisposed' in his home. This practice was originally begun to give the new chief a chance to ensconce himself firmly on the throne before any aspiring contender had a chance to organise some opposition.

This happened when Senzangakona died. In the period when news of his death was secret, his son Sigujana quietly took his place and by the time Shaka heard about his father's death, Sigujana was already in the saddle.

INTRODUCTION TO THE ZULU

Typical Zulu country seen from the northern end of the Valley of a Thousand Hills. The Tugela River – boundary of the old Zululand – lies in the distance.

On the banks of the historic Tugela river on a warm, dry winter's day. In the summer rainy season the water would have been close up on my left.

Mandawe Hill, 14 km north of Eshowe. On its lower slope, Malandela the progenitor of the Zulu nation, long ago, made his home with his family, which included a young son named Zulu . . . the boy who later gave his name to the Nation.

The country Zulu are by nature agriculturalists. They love their cattle, which are not only a source of milk and meat but are the medium by which the men acquire their wives. The cultivated lands in this tranquil country scene are used for maize crops.

Gnu or Blue Wildebeest in Natal's Mkuzi Game Reserve. The tail brush of these animals is much sought after by Zulu Diviners (witch-doctors) among whom a brush attached to a small handle of wood is a symbol of their office and an essential part of their sacred equipment.

While huts are invariably domed in shape they are not always completely 'grassed' down to the ground because this is a fire hazard when the family makes a fire indoors. These are homes deep in the Mhlatuze River valley.

The techniques and skills of hut-making and thatching varies among the numerous clans which make the Zulu nation. This scene is at the foot of the beautiful Drakensberg.

Left: Pack-donkeys are often used to carry produce to be sold to a trader and for goods purchased from him.

Right: A cow of the hardy Nguni breed which has come down with the Zulu through many generations. They are easily recognisable by the shape of their horns.

An interesting gathering of men and women I met at a kraal in the Tugela Ferry area. They are, from the left standing: a tanner and leather-worker; a medicine-man (*nyanga*) – in his assortment of horns and bottles he carries his medicines; the head of the host-kraal with his ceremonial shield and head-dress; a married woman with the head-dress common in her clan; a girl dressed in her special party beads. Sitting, the elderly lady is a diviner (witch-doctor) and next to her is the assistant or trainee of the medicine man who is standing.

24

In fine weather the people of the kraals often cook out of doors in preference to using their kitchens or living huts and their domestic animals invariably gather round for pickings.

26

28   Styles in dress, among women and girls of the country kraals are often localised within specific clans or territorial areas. The women here are of the ancient Ntombela clan.

The colours of beads and type of pieces worn by a girl often identifies her clan. This girl is of the Mabaso to the north of Tugela Ferry.

Any age is an age for dancing among the Zulu and any occasion is a good occasion.

A girl and her young friend watch in intense admiration through the smoke of the kraal fire.

Shining with perspiration and panting, a dancer drops down to rest.

A draft of beer never goes amiss after strenuous exercise but a little miss watches – it seems critically – in the background.

32   A young courting couple of the Cele clan meet at dusk. A ceremonial shield is invariably carried by men in their going-out dress. To be really fashionable girls carry a black rolled umbrella.

Dingiswayo Supports Shaka	Shaka was furious and Dingiswayo, his protector and the overlord of the Zulu clan, felt that in the absence of a publicly announced successor by the late Zulu chief he, Dingiswayo, had the right to choose the successor to the Zulu chieftaincy. But Dingiswayo was a born statesman and reluctant to take sides openly. Nevertheless, Shaka knew where he stood and made his own plans to have the new chief removed. He enlisted the help of his half-brother Ngwadi to do the spadework. He was Shaka's mother's son born to a father named Ngendeyana who cared for Nandi and Shaka at one stage after their expulsion from the royal Zulu household. He was of the Mbedwini clan.

The two brothers had a close relationship and Ngwadi agreed to befriend the new Zulu chief, gain his trust and then kill him. Sigujana, the chief, got to like his new friend and went with him to the river in the mornings to wash. This was how Ngwadi had planned it. He hid two accomplices with assegais in the trees beside the river, and before long their weapons both ended in the chief's back.

Shaka Returns Home

It seems uncertain as to how long Sigujana ruled. It could have been a few weeks, or even months, because at that time the Zulu embalmed their chiefs by encasing them in the hide of a freshly slaughtered ox and then sitting them in front of a fire in their hut to dry out. Only after this had been done could they be buried, because their bodies were no longer of any use to witches who might otherwise have dug them up for magic medicine. So in the apparent absence of any certainty as to how long it was before Senzangakona was buried or before Sigujana publicly came into the open as the new leader, the period of his rule cannot be fixed. But in any event it was shortlived.

Shaka's reaction when he received the news that his brother was dead, was like a whirlwind. He marched back to his original home, the chief's royal kraal, with a specially chosen bodyguard given him by King Dingiswayo, his patron and protector, and left no challenger or contender in any doubt that he had come to stay.

It was, however, patently obvious that his younger half-brother Dingane was acutely jealous and unhappy. He was at this stage not influential enough to offer any opposition to Shaka, but history has shown that in his own time and in his own way and goaded by a burning ambition, he was to play a role which vitally influenced the course of events in Southern Africa.

Birth of the Warriors

Without any softening-up process, Shaka climbed straight into the saddle. His first objective was an army and he began to train every available male in his tiny population of seventeen hundred souls to fight with the new short-handle *stabbing* spear which he had pioneered. Up to now, tribesmen had fought with a handful of flimsy, long-handled *throwing* spears, but Shaka ridiculed the idea that any man should 'throw his weapons away'. So his warriors carried a single spear and a club and were trained to fight to the death with them if necessary. Any man who lost his spear in battle and lost his fight was invariably executed and so lost his life too. Shaka was fanatical about physical fitness and as an aid to his hand-to-hand fighting, he trained his men to be fleet of foot and agile in their movements. This was essential not only in combat but for pursuit and to this end he made his warriors discard their sandals and fight bare-footed. He eventually also had regiments of girls, but they were not used in open combat.

Shaka's ambition was conquest, and his objective was a kingdom and an empire where his word would be supreme.

It is often said that his driving force was born out of the inferiority complex he developed as a child in his years of hardship and that it gave him an eternal desire to prove his strength.

In any event, whatever his motivation, he had intelligence, determination, the strength of will and the physique to support it.

In common with their other Nguni brother-tribesmen, the Zulu of the kraal love long hours of lazing in the sun with nothing better than gossip to occupy their day. Shaka came like an explosion, bursting in on their lethargy. He got them to their feet and running. He whipped life and action into them before they had time to rub the sleep from their eyes.

He harnessed both his superior intelligence and his indefatigable energy to establish himself as someone of force and power in the land. He had a splendid body which left no enemy in doubt of the danger of facing him in combat. His iron discipline was simple to those it concerned: either their loyalty or their death. He was a tireless worker, but he needed elbow room because the Zulu realm he inherited was only sixteen by sixteen kilometres in size, and even that lay under the ultimate sovereignty of his old patron master – King Dingiswayo of the Mtetwa.

The Zulu at that time were just another of the numerous clans which had evolved out of the same original Natal Nguni bloodstock. They were no different in nature or character from any of their neighbours.

Up to Shaka's time, wars between the clans had been disorderly affairs with opposing forces lined up throwing assegais at each other, while their womenfolk watched on the sides and egged them on. The combatants kept the battle going by grabbing up the fallen spears thrown at them and hurling them back. They carried only modest-sized shields and wore cowhide sandals. Casualties in these fights were negligible compared with those which were to follow at Shaka's hands.

When he took up the reigns as chief of the Zulu clan, Shaka also took command of the life of each of his men and soon the individual, as such, was deprived of his role as a normal family man. Instead, he became part of the Zulu war instrument, was encamped in military garrisons and could not marry before Shaka allowed him to do so at the age of approximately thirty-five years and even then only after he had earned this privilege in battle.

Military Training

Shaka's military training was rigorous. His first move was to abolish the use of sandals, because they slowed a warrior up and impeded his footwork in hand-to-hand battle. This caused near riots in the beginning, because it needed really tough feet to stand up to the country's rugged ground. But Shaka hardened his own feet to take the punishment and expected everyone else to do the same. When there was mumbling in the ranks because of his 'bare-feet' order he took immediate action. He ordered an assembly and covered his parade ground with triple-spiked 'devil-thorns'. These formidable little creations are known in Afrikaans as '*duiweltjies*' (little devils) and in Zulu as '*nkunzana*' (little bulls) but no matter what their name they are one of nature's most devastating devices to walk on. At the parade Shaka ordered his men to stamp the thorns well into the parade ground 'to give it a good surface'!

Howls of pain and protest followed but Shaka was unmoved. He showed his men exactly *how* they had to stamp the thorns in and then had half a dozen of those who had cried the loudest clubbed to death for effect. The rest tackled

34

their job with relish and agreed with Shaka that it made them 'feel good'! After this episode they limped only when their chief was not around.

In all his life Shaka was never conventional if he could be original. But at the same time he always calculated the effect of his moves in advance. For their part, his subjects learned never to question his word unless he invited it and in this way he instilled into them a special discipline which is still obvious today. In respect of character he bred into them honesty of a particularly high order and anyone who stole a cow or raped a woman, for instance, was executed immediately.

The Crossroads Any outsider surveying the scene in Nguniland in the year 1816 and speculating about its future, would have found an intriguing situation with the odds heavily against him picking the winner from the three contenders who at that time were struggling for supremacy.

Each one of these emergent leaders would probably have been capable of leading the people along his chosen path and of fusing the various clans into a nation, but in the case of two of them, only a guess can be hazarded as to what sort of nation would have emerged or what its future would have been. The tribes in 1816 were thus at the crossroads. Physically, the people had ample room to graze their cattle and to grow their corn and to hunt happily, but space was not the issue. In fact I am prepared to suggest that they, the tribespeople themselves, wanted nothing new at all so long as their next meal was handy and they were allowed to sit in the sun and chat. But that was not to be because these three strong-willed men were all then grasping for power and aggrandisement at the same time in different clans, and their struggle dominated the course of history during the next decade.

I mentioned earlier how the population of the land was made up of many clans, some big and some small, but without overall cohesion. At the time of Shaka's advent in 1816, a few strong tribes had emerged, like the Qwabe whose founder was the brother of the original patriarch Zulu. There were others, like the Cunu and the Ngcobo, but the two strongest were the Ndwandwe under a wily and treacherous chief named Zwide, and the Mtetwa under Dingiswayo who was a fine ruler, but too trusting. Both chiefs had swallowed up several of their neighbouring tribes and had become kings in their own right. In 1816 the two of them were at each other's throats in a bid to gain the ultimate and final supremacy of all Nguniland. Shaka Zulu was hardly more than a fledgling in the background at this time; his following was still small and his situation was complicated further by the fact that not only was he Dingiswayo's friend and ally but he was also vassal to him and subject to his overlordship.

It would have seemed certain, therefore, that the future of the land had to lie in the hands of one of the first two, that is, Zwide or Dingiswayo. To have bet on Shaka of the Zulu at that stage, would, to say the least, have been premature.

Looking back now in retrospect, the path of events leading up to the climax in Nguniland was full of surprises and unexpected turns.

Shaka Sets Course While Shaka's military strength was minimal in the beginning, he, the man, was conspicuous by his originality and initiative. It can be claimed that he was a man born ahead of his era with faculties which gave him a distinct advantage in leadership among the primitive people of his time. He schemed and planned and his moves were always one jump ahead of his adversaries who could seldom anticipate them. His first expansionistic move was also an illustration of his initiative and strategy. He wanted more warriors but did not wish to lose any that he already had by involving them in open conflict. So he planned a surprise move to subjugate the Langeni Chief Makedama. Unexpectedly, at dawn one morning, Shaka's warriors surrounded Makedama's kraal as well as those of one or two others of his senior counsellors and called on them all to surrender. Caught completely off guard, Makedama had little choice, nor did he have any wish to die prematurely. He not only gave in, but promised complete allegiance to Shaka and even offered to contribute to his army. With this promise extracted from him, the Langeni chief was allowed to retain his seat, and with it his clan could thus keep its individuality and pride. Shaka had taken an important step and now controlled two clans, the Zulu and the Langeni. As in this case, Shaka, in his later conquests, followed the far-sighted policy of allowing old chiefs who promised their allegiance to stay in their seats. Where, however, a conquered chief would not submit to his will or betrayed him, Shaka usually destroyed him and at times his entire clan with him.

The conquest of the Langeni was admittedly not an exhibition of heroics. It was, nevertheless, a fearless show of strength by Shaka, because after the surrender he immediately held a trial of people in the clan who had displeased him in his childhood, or who had been unkind to his mother, Nandi. She, it will be remembered, was born a Langeni but had suffered their displeasure because of her love-affair which resulted in Shaka's birth.

At the trial Shaka summarily sentenced about two dozen Langeni to instant death. He allowed those with 'lesser crimes' the 'privilege' of a quick death by clubbing, but those who had displeased him to a greater extent were impaled on the sharpened poles in the fence of a cattle byre. In Shaka's chosen time the fence was later set alight by executioners to shorten the misery of the victims. As they died, the victims shouted the royal salute of 'Bayede!' to their 'father, Chief Shaka'. Such was the man Shaka and such the character and loyalty of the Zulu who believe that 'a chief can do no wrong'. One thing a Zulu specifically respects and admires is strength. He stoically accepts the most severe punishment from his leader because, by tradition, his word is law. What he says is final.

Shaka's little expedition to the Langeni put an aura around him and brought young men from several neighbouring clans clamouring to join his warrior ranks to share the glory they offered. Many, of course, also hoped for fame for themselves. Other young men were even sent by friendly neighbouring chiefs to serve with Shaka. They trained daily and hard, and apart from combat tactics learned discipline and the need for self-control. Shaka punished disobedience and even minor deviations with immediate death by an executioner who was constantly at his side with a club or a spear.

The bodies of these unfortunate victims were rarely buried but were abandoned in the veld or bush to be disposed of by nature's anti-pollution agents in the form of scavenging jackals, hyaenas and vultures. Only very important persons, such as chiefs, were actually buried. Despite all, Shaka's warriors idolised him – in his first years at any rate.

Shaka Tests his Warriors

The young army was soon ready for a physical trial of strength and Shaka chose the Buthelezi clan as his objective because he had a score to settle with their chief, Pungashe.

In the time of Senzangakona, Shaka's father, Pungashe had periodically clashed with the Zulu in faction fights and won. In these clashes the Zulu chief, Senzangakona, was often taken captive by the Buthelezi and had to be ransomed by his wives with cattle before the Buthelezi would release him. Shaka remembered these incidents and he yearned for revenge but waited for the ideal opportunity. This presented itself eventually in the form of personal insults directed by Pungashe at Shaka 'the pup'. Foolishly Pungashe also derided Shaka's so-called military strength. This was all Shaka needed.

War was declared quite conventionally with neither side trying any surprises on the other. The two sides drew up on the battlefield face to face, with a no-man's-land between them.

The Buthelezi had their fists full of long-handled throwing spears and the Zulu had a single, short-handled, broad-bladed spear and a club each. Both sides had their shields, but Shaka's were bigger, being in the region of some one hundred and twenty centimetres (4 ft.) tall.

Pungashe sat on a hill behind his troops to watch the fight and the 'fun' while Shaka led his men himself. Buthelezi women came to watch and cheer and praise. In customary tribal fashion the Buthelezi threw insults and threats across no-man's-land, but Shaka's trained men were unmoved by this goading. His law was that they acted on *orders* only and anyone who lost his self-control would be punished, most likely with death.

The battle began in a shower of Buthelezi spears but the Zulu were prepared and easily warded them off with their shields. Then Shaka unleashed his men in what became his famous 'buffalo horns' manoeuvre. He sent a column racing past on each side of the enemy in a move to come in from their sides and back to encircle them. Then he hit straight from the front with the 'buffalo's chest' in man-to-man combat. The long Buthelezi spears were unwieldy and useless as the Zulu slashed and stabbed with blood-thirsty relish with their short weapons.

Chief Pungashe fled and his men were cut to ribbons. Women suffered the same fate. In chasing those who escaped, the Zulu sacked and burned the Buthelezi kraals, and as they passed dead warriors slashed open their stomachs to free their spirits. Disembowelling of dead men left on the battlefield was practised by all black warriors of the time in the belief that this would set free the spirits imprisoned inside their distended abdomens.

After the battle the Zulu assisted any of their own men who could still benefit from help, but they stabbed in the heart those who were desperately wounded to save them from suffering. This practice was approved by injured warriors themselves and was common procedure. The enemy wounded were all killed, irrespective of their degree of injury.

After this battle the Buthelezi clan was taken under Shaka's wing and served him with pride and as a great leader. There was no rancour.

Shaka and Dingiswayo

And so Shaka's following grew. But conqueror though he was, he was still subservient to his erstwhile protector and benefactor, King Dingiswayo of the Mtetwa. But the king did not object to Shaka's growing power because he was an ally and formed a barrier between the Mtetwa and possible enemies. He also intended to call on Shaka to help him silence his old enemy Zwide, of the Ndwandwe, when the time came, as it must.

In 1818, after Shaka had been in the saddle for two years, the feud between

Nguniland's two traditional enemies continued. Up to then Dingiswayo had captured the treacherous Zwide three times, but had foolishly released him each time with the admonition that he should behave himself! Dingiswayo's enlightened behaviour, however, was not in keeping with the savagery of the times and he would eventually have to pay dearly for it.

Despite Shaka's repeated warning to him never to let an enemy live to 'come at you a second time', Dingiswayo never learned his lesson.

Witchcraft on Dingiswayo

Zwide for his part now had a cunning inspiration. He decided to ensnare his old enemy by casting a magic spell over him, and in this way get him under his power. With this in mind he therefore called in his best medicine men.

At this stage of the story, I think it is necessary to deviate for a moment to explain one of the most interesting tribal beliefs about magic medicine. It is firmly believed that in order to make the best medicine for bewitching someone, something personal from the intended victim's body must be obtained such as his sweat, or dirt from under his feet, or his hair. The more intimate the personal ingredient, the more potent the medicine will be. It is not always easy for a medicine man to obtain this primary element from the person whom he hopes to bewitch, but once this has been done, he mixes it into a concoction of his own ingredients perhaps even including items like rat-droppings or dried bats' wings. Then he doctors the whole lot so that the brew will create a spell of the particular kind he wants for his victim. The Zulu theory about the necessity for the *personal* ingredient in the medicine is that, when it has been appropriately treated, it sends out 'homing' impulses or 'attractions' to the 'parent' from which it came and that this person's body in turn feels the communication and responds in sympathy in a way in which the maker designed. If the medicine is strong enough, the spell it casts takes over the body competely and then *controls* it – apparently without the subject being aware of his actions.

This is how Zwide planned to get Dingiswayo into his power and in his scheming he was supported by his mother, Ntombazi, a self-confessed witch who was intensely ambitious for her son. All concerned were in agreement that the most potent ingredient to use in the making of the medicine was some of Dingiswayo's own sperm but the question was *how* to get it. With this in mind, Zwide called in his sister, Ntombazana ('little Ntombazi'). Legend has it that she was beautiful. She must, furthermore, have inherited some of her mother's skills in witchcraft, for she agreed to go to Dingiswayo's court and use her guile to get herself seduced by him. She was successful in her mission and returned to the medicine makers with their requirement and they, in turn, jubilantly set to and brewed the fatal mixture.

With the stage set, Zwide, a little recklessly, put all his faith in his magical plan and rather too little into his military preparations. His next step was to get Dingiswayo within his reach and with this in view he started a chain of goading incidents to lure his old enemy into another fight and a trap.

The outcome of it all was like a fairy-tale or, perhaps better, an ogre-tale. It is almost beyond human understanding but the story is probably no more mysterious than many others which come out of Zulu kraals.

Dingiswayo was taunted by Zwide beyond his patience and took the bait. He gathered his own army and arranged for Shaka to join him at a given spot from where they would then head for Ndwandweland, up near the Black Mfolozi River. It all looked as if Zwide had exposed himself to a risky gamble because he had already lost several times to Dingiswayo in battle and this time Shaka would also be there with his Zulu contingent.

The Spell at Work

Then strange things began to happen. For a start, a fault in communications with Shaka upset their rendezvous; then, at the point were Dingiswayo's army expected to make contact with the Ndwandwe, everything was quiet; too quiet. But this was according to Zwide's plan because Dingiswayo had entered into the zone where he had laid the magic spell.

At this point Dingiswayo, the great warrior king, all at once changed. Inexplicably, he went into what must have been a trance and became remote and apparently quite unconscious of anything around him. His mind must have been taken over. Without reason, or apparent reasoning, he began to walk. He went straight ahead alone, except for a small group of Zulu girl-attendants who hurried to his side. Without any hesitation Dingiswayo walked on until he stumbled into an outpost of Ndwandwe warriors who took him, without resistance, straight to the kraal of his jubilant enemy, Zwide, and his mother Ntombazi, who kept a museum of the skulls of conquered chiefs. There, they shut him up in a hut with his faithful following of girls, and in a while he regained his normal senses and all the dignity of the great man that he was.

Zwide ordered cattle to be killed 'in honour' of his royal 'guest' and a feast was held. Then, in the midst of it all, with his usual brutality, and prompted by his mother, Zwide ordered his executioners to kill his old rival King Dingiswayo of the Mtetwa. They obeyed. Zwide offered Dingiswayo's girls their freedom and an escort to take them back home, but they disdained the choice and stabbed themselves to death so that they fell to cover their master's body with their own as a last supreme act of loyalty to him.

The Aftermath

It is logical to wonder, on thinking of this incident, *why* Dingiswayo's army did not come to their leader's rescue in his hour of peril. As an answer I cannot do better than quote the eminent authority on the Zulu, Dr A. T. Bryant. He says: 'That the Mtetwa army heretofore, so consistently victorious over every clan, should thus have failed in the supreme moment valiantly to respond to the call of its captured king, can only be attributed to the innate helplessness of the Bantu people when once deprived of their leader. Individually incapable of initiative and independent action, they develop will-power and energy only when collected in the mass, unless there arises one stronger than the rest to lead the way. Like sheep, they will follow a strong leader blindly, even over the precipice unto certain death; but left alone, they will stand idle and helpless or be scattered by the ravening wolf.'

Zwide rejoiced and perhaps gave too much time to this immediate personal victory over his old enemy and not enough to strategic planning for the next step. At this moment there seemed to be little that could prevent him from wearing the crown of emperor of all Nguniland and ruling over every clan and tribe in it. A leader must have the quality to think quickly in all circumstances and Zwide should have done the logical thing immediately and thrown his whole fighting force into battle against the now leaderless, confused and suspicion-racked Mtwetwa warriors who were still far from home and crushed them. But he had not backed up his magic with adequate military planning or preparation. The Ndwandwe army did, in fact, pursue the Mtetwa well on their way home, but at the crucial moment, when victory was within their reach,

Zwide learned that Shaka and his men had arrived on the flank of his territory and so he hurriedly recalled his warriors from the chase to counter the Zulu threat.

Shaka, for his part, had been on his way through the Kumalo clan territory to meet Dingiswayo when their young chief, Donda, told him of Dingiswayo's death and by so doing saved Shaka from certain disaster. Shaka immediately withdrew his forces to safety, but, sadly, Donda was destined to pay heavily for his action.

Zwide's Revenge

The land of Zwide's Ndwandwe was in the north of Nguniland near Nongoma and the Black Mfolozi River and Donda's Kumalo people formed a barrier to their south, between them and the Zulu. The young Kumalo chief was too friendly with Shaka for Zwide's liking and this latest incident gave him all the incentive he needed – if he needed any at all – to prompt him in his next treacherous scheme. I feel justified in saying here that the pattern of deceitful scheming shown by Zwide is not a characteristic of the average men of the kraals. In fact, to my mind, they despise treachery as something loathesome. They can be rugged, blood-thirsty and warlike, yes, but cunning underhandedness is not something which they admire. They would rather have a straight fight.

His conscience, however, did not worry Zwide. If Donda was an obstacle to his expansionistic programme, then Donda would have to be removed in a way that suited Zwide best. So, with ugly cunning, he invited the young Kumalo chief and a group of his young men to join him in a wild-game hunt. In issuing the invitation he told Donda and his party that they need bring only light hunting spears and that shields were not necessary. He mentioned also that after the hunt there would be a love-dance and that the Kumalo men should bring girls with them. A token hunt *did* take place, but at the end of it the Ndwandwe surrounded Donda and his men and killed every one of them and then carried the girls off.

Ntombazi, Zwide's evil mother, took Chief Donda's head to add to her collection. She believed that by collecting the heads of vanquished chiefs and dignatories, she would have the essence of their power in her hands and with the aid of magic would be able to add that power to the strength of their conqueror – her son, Zwide.

Ritual Murder

This idea of absorbing someone else's strength is common among many of South Africa's black people. It has led to many a ritual murder among them and still does, even in this so-called modern age. It happens, for instance, when some influential person feels that he would like a particular characteristic which someone else has and he lacks. To get it, it is commonly believed that the person wanting it must be doctored with the relative parts of a person who has the desired characteristic. So a murder happens and a diviner (witchdoctor) or a herbalist, who is prepared to do so (or a witch), makes the magic medicine and treats the client with it. The medicine may be applied in several ways. For instance, the person may take it physically or wash down his body with it in the light of the rising sun. It depends largely on the practitioner's instructions. It must be made clear, though, that not every diviner or herbalist by any means, would be prepared to dabble in such a nefarious practice as ritual murder.

Sometimes, the sought-after characteristics are in an animal and then the course is easier. For instance, if a man wants to be fleet of foot, like a springbok, then all he has to do is to get the leg muscles of a springbok and eat them, either alone or in a magic brew. Alternately, if he wishes to be 'strong with women' like the impala antelope, which sires many does, then he eats the male organs of the impala and so on.

An interesting fact about ritual murders of people is that the victim's family might find out or know who the murderer or his 'employer' is, but they will seldom, if ever, report him to the police or admit that they know anything. They are so bound by superstition and fear of supernatural consequences to themselves, that they keep quiet and deny any knowledge they may have.

Enter Mzilikazi

It is now necessary to return momentarily to Zwide, who was not satisfied with only the death of the Kumalo chief, Donda, but set his sights on another branch of the clan further to the north-east near Mkuze. Its chief was actually Zwide's own son-in-law – but this made no difference to him. The man was Mashobana Kumalo, father of Mzilikazi, who was later to achieve fame through his conquests of northern territories and his founding of the Matabele nation in Rhodesia.

Without sentiment or mercy, Zwide sent his men against this second branch of the clan and they brought Mashobana's head back to queen Ntombazi for her museum. Mashobana's son, Mzilikazi Kumalo, was spared but he and his people were made vassals of their conqueror. It did not require all of Mzilikaze's great intelligence to realise that his head would be safer if it were further away from his grandfather and great-grandmother and so, with a small following, he pulled up his roots and sought refuge with Shaka who instantly realised that here was a young man of exceptional calibre and potential. Mzilikazi soon rose to be a general in Shaka's army and later went on to create his own fame in far-distant fields.

Qokli Hill

With the exciting memory of his victory over Dingiswayo still tingling in his veins, Zwide now decided to settle scores with Shaka and get him out of the way. This was at the beginning of 1818 and he had about twelve thousand formidable warriors available. Shaka's strength had been reinforced by many of the leaderless Mtetwa who had come to join him, but it still only numbered about five thousand men. They were, however, brilliant in-fighters, trained by Shaka's renowned warrior friend named Mgobozi.

Battle was inevitable and when it came, took the form of one of the most dramatic and decisive events in the history of Nguniland. Qokli Hill, where the opposing forces met in battle, is visible on the east side of the main road from Melmoth to Ulundi at a point within reasonable walking distance from the present bridge over the White Mfolozi River.

I have climbed Qokli Hill myself. It is a rugged, rough and formidable battlefield. It brought to my mind thoughts of ferocity and bravery and of sacrifices which were almost too severe and dramatic to translate into reality. Here a nation was born.

An important feature of the hill is that it overlooks the drift where the Ndwandwe, in their approach had to cross the Mfolozi River. On the hill, Shaka knew in advance every move the enemy made because apart from what he could see, he was kept well informed by his intelligence service of their every move.

Cleverly, Shaka had lured the Ndwandwe to this, his own battleground and with careful forethought had laid all his plans in advance. One of the trump cards in his strategy was his plan to deprive the enemy of water in the field. He did this by mobilising his men on top of Qokli Hill which was far away enough from the river to ensure that in the heat of battle, Ndwandwe warriors would continually have to break off in large numbers and go in search of water to quench their thirst in the hot and dehydrating climate of the area. With calculated forethought, Shaka, who was personally in command, laid in large stores of water and food on top of his hill for his men. Zwide, his enemy, stayed safely at home and gave the command of the Ndwandwe to his son, Nomahlanjana, who was accompanied by four of his brother princes.

From his chosen site on the hilltop the Zulu chief carefully watched the enemy approach, and at a strategic time had a herd of his cattle driven off as a decoy within their view. This caused an excited stir in the invaders' ranks and their commander immediately took the bait and sent a large contingent of his men after the cattle. This was just what Shaka wanted, but he was still outnumbered by three to one because he had to let a good number of his own men go with the cattle to protect them. Shaka concentrated a limited number of his warriors in open view on the crest of Qokli Hill to deceive the enemy and then hid a strong reserve force on the slope at the back of the hill.

The Ndwandwe leader made his first mistake by initially forming up his lines of warriors across a wide front on a plain below the hill. Qokli Hill is round and the higher the warriors climbed the shorter their frontage became until eventually they were unable to manoeuvre their long-handled throwing spears in the confined space left to them.

With the calm that characterised Shaka, he allowed the advance to come dangerously close and not one of his men moved. Then, at the crucial psychological moment, he let them loose like a bolt of pent-up lightning. Their uncluttered bare feet carried them down on to the solid wall of enemy warriors ahead like water through a broken dyke. Their broad stabbing blades speared into the living mass.

The Ndwandwe were used to fighting enemies who *threw* spears as they did, so that both sides were able to pick up weapons continuously. Instead of doing this, Shaka's men once again fought close-in using their stabbing spears as they had done against the Buthelezi and in addition they wielded heavy clubs with devastating results. And almost worse, Shaka had young carrier boys racing about picking up fallen spears to deprive the Ndwandwe of any further use of them.

Shaka personally kept an iron discipline on his men throughout the two days of battle but, at one stage, a group of them got carried away in the heat of battle and ran into a trap when they chased an enemy contingent which pretended to flee. Caught, the Zulu had to fight desperately to escape. Shaka was furious, but was great enough to praise them for their brave fight. Even though he could not afford to lose any of his fighting men, he knew that he could not let them go unpunished, so he sent six of them out to face the enemy alone and fight until they each died.

The six walked out bravely, turned and gave Shaka the royal salute of 'Bayede!' and fought like demons.

'Buffalo Horns'

No Shakan battle was ever complete without his 'buffalo horns' movement.
With the Qokli Hill battle at a high pitch on the second day, the enemy

42

leader, Nomahlanjana, suddenly changed his tactics. He sent a column like a battering ram straight up the hill at Shaka. It was about twenty men wide and two hundred metres from front to back. Shaka was delighted. It was a gift from his ancestors. He quickly brought up a large contingent of fresh warriors concealed on the southern slope of Qokli, behind him. He put them into two long columns, eight abreast, and sent one racing down each side of the Ndwandwe mass. They were his 'buffalo horns'. In a shock move, he then threw his main force, his 'buffalo chest', straight at the head of the Ndwandwe battering ram coming towards him.

The carnage and violence was indescribable, but suffice it to say that men like these fought with no thought of self. Their chief came first and death was a contribution to his cause. But they never gave their lives easily because that would be failing him and a disgrace to his prestige.

The 'horns' reached the far-end of the Ndwandwe column and began to close on each side of it. Seeing what was happening, and in a panic, the Ndwandwe commander, Nomahlanjana, hoping for protection rushed in to join his men because he could see no escape in running in any other direction. The horns closed behind him. His men in the centre of the twenty-wide corps were useless because they could not fight until their comrades at their sides fell, then they had to fight over their bodies.

Nomahlanjana and his four brother princes – all sons of King Zwide – died fighting. The remaining men in the column turned and tried to fight their way out along the pathway by which they had come and they all died too. The entire column of fifteen hundred men perished. Shaka lost about five hundred.

Victory and a Kingdom

If there was any specific hour or day in which the multi-tribal land of the Natal Nguni became Zululand and a united kingdom, this was it. But the kingdom nearly died at birth on that same day because Shaka made a mistake. With the battering ram of the Ndwandwe decimated, he decided to follow up and destroy the many stragglers who had gone in search of water or had otherwise become detached in the fighting. Shaka personally joined in the hunt.

In the chase that followed, the Zulu warriors ran headlong into a large Ndwandwe contingent coming back from following Shaka's decoy cattle. Shaka had only a handful of men with him, because a brigade, which he called the Belebele, was hunting Ndwandwe in another direction. The Zulu chief was in deadly peril, but somehow managed to extricate his men. Then, fighting a rearguard action, he was driven back to the very gates of his own royal kraal of Bulawayo. He made a stand there in the desperate hope of salvaging his 'Great Place' from the torches of the enemy.

With his broad blade and great white shield with one black dot on it, he fought at the side of his men and rallied them wherever they needed it most. The very heart of the Zulu was exposed and the future was in the balance.

Then – in their most critical hour – help came. The Belebele Brigade returned from 'mopping-up' and attacked the enemy in the back. It was a pincer movement – a 'buffalo horns' of another kind.

With victory within their grasp, and their hands closing around the Zulu throat, the Ndwandwe were once again trapped. Those who could escape fled homewards. Those who were less fortunate died. The battle of Qokli Hill was over. Zwide lost five sons and seven and a half thousand warriors in this, his first open conflict with Shaka Zulu.

It had, none the less, cost Shaka a heavy battering and his fighting force was reduced to a bare thousand and a half men. If it had not been for the genius that was this man, and the help of fate, none at all would have lived to carry the Zulu banner into the pages of history. The Zulu nation would have died at birth on that day in April 1818.

Chapter 2
The Warrior King

The Zulu love a hero and there was none greater than Shaka after the battle of Qokli Hill. His name echoed down the valleys and across the hills. The Zulu also love a strong leader and in need they will stoically die for him.

Men came from many sides to join the ranks of Shaka's warriors and he made treaties with friendly neighbouring chiefs to get others from their clans. They were all trained relentlessly and Shaka promoted those who proved their ability and leadership qualities to the top ranks irrespective of the clans of their origin. This absence of any favouritism towards men of his own clan showed good sense on Shaka's part not only because in this way he got the best leaders but also because his policy resulted in fusing the different clans of his army into a composite united body with a common cause.

Shaka's Year of Grace

Despite the battering he had given the Ndwandwe, Shaka knew that Zwide's bruised ego and pride would never let him rest, nor would his mother Ntombazi, the witch who was determined to add Shaka's scalp to her collection. But there was one factor in Shaka's favour. Because of the five princes of the royal Ndwandwe household who fell at Qokli Hill, he would have at least a year's grace in which to prepare. It is tribal custom that when a kraal head or senior man dies, then his family keeps a rigid ritual of mourning in which they may not, for a time, till their lands, eat certain foods or do certain types of work. If a chief dies then his whole clan is similarly affected – they virtually grind to a halt for a long period while they follow numerous taboos. At Qokli Hill five of the Ndwandwe king's sons died and the Zulu knew that mourning would go on for at least 'twelve moons'. This would affect both recruiting and training and would bring the army to a standstill. It did, but Zwide, as king ruling over a large number of clans in the north of Nguniland, had a big reservoir of young men to call upon to rebuild his ranks when the time ultimately came for reprisals against Shaka.

Sanctuary for the Mtetwa

A particularly important change in Shaka's relationship with his old friends, the Mtetwa, now came about. After their chief, Dingiswayo, was murdered the Mtetwa found themselves leaderless, afraid and in a wilderness of superstition. But Qokli Hill erased their dilemma. They saw a chance of protection ahead and a wing under which they could 'find shade'.

It would perhaps be a little unfair to suggest that at that moment they became *vassal* to the still tiny Zulu kingdom, though they did throw in their lot with the Zulu and Shaka, who was certainly a dominating figure in the federation. Shaka appointed an old boyhood friend named Mlandela* as chief of the Mtetwa tribe as such, and another Mtetwa tribesman, Ngomane, as his own Zulu Prime Minister.

*Not to be confused with Malandela, father of Zulu.

My reference to 'Zulu' now is, of course, to the Zulu *Nation* because as Shaka absorbed other clans and tribes into his kingdom, they became Zulu even though it was not his normal policy to deprive them of their own clan identities or *sibongo*. These they retained.

The Clan Name

In case my use above of single first-names when referring to the leaders of that time is confusing, I should explain that this is customary everyday usage among the Zulu people. If there is ever any doubt as to *which* Ngomane, for example, is referred to, they identify him as 'son-of-so-and-so' who was the 'son-of-so-and-so'. One reason why a surname or family name (*sibongo*) is not as a rule used more frequently, is that clans generally live grouped together in specific areas under their own chieftains and, of course, have the same clan names or 'surnames'. If an individual should move to a different area he might easily, in the beginning anyway, quote himself as (for instance) 'Mvula kwaNtombela'. This means that his first name is *Mvula* and he is of the Ntombela clan.

The Shakan Mould

With the developments I have mentioned, Shaka grew in stature and in these early years he was idolised even though he showed little feeling for human life. But then, the Zulu respect their chief to the extent that 'he can do no wrong'. Shaka moulded a definite character into his people and, if there were any particular aspects of it which dominated the rest, they were those of loyalty to him and to the Zulu race. Then they learned discipline, including self-discipline as probably few tribes have.

An example of the self-discipline which Shaka imposed can be found in the attitude he adopted towards the 'Wiping of the Axe' or the 'Washing of the Spear' ceremony. This is the cleansing ceremony for a returning warrior who has killed someone in battle. Part of the ceremony prescribes that the warrior must have intercourse with the first girl he meets on his way home, but it must be *external* contact only. The Zulu call it *hlobonga* and in it the man may not take the maiden's virginity. If Shaka found that any man had broken this law, he fined him in cattle or executed him instantly. These codes of honour which he instilled into his people have come down in their character through subsequent generations of Zulu to the present time.

War Clouds

But I must return to the adventures of the warrior king. By mid-1819, that is not much more than a year after the battle of Qokli Hill, Shaka had rebuilt his army from the fifteen hundred survivors to ten thousand men. This was only three years after he originally took over the chieftaincy of the Zulu clan which at that time numbered in total only seventeen hundred men, women and children. Zwide, for his part, had boosted his ranks to eighteen thousand men and at their head he put the clever and subsequently famous Soshangane. The two mighty armies were ready for battle.

Shakan Strategy

Shaka was unschooled and without any knowledge of reading or writing. His people were primitive and knew nothing of the civilised world beyond their horizon and Shaka's own first real contact with the white man was only in 1825 by which time he, Shaka, already held the new Zulu nation trembling in the cup of his hand. But Mother Nature had endowed him at birth with rare qualities which helped to shape his destiny as a man and helped him overcome what he lacked in academic knowledge.

He had a superior intellect from which ideas were born that were far in advance of his era and he innovated schemes which were completely out of context with the times and circumstances in which he lived. Among these was his establishment of an efficient secret service which he used in his army and which was invaluable to him in his military strategy. In the early years when his warriors were numerically outnumbered by those of his enemies, he had a desperate need for information and his secret service not only kept him up to date with details of the preparations for battle against him, but it also fed his enemy, Zwide, with false information about Shaka's preparations for war. A key figure in Shaka's service at that time was a man named Noluju. The latter had gained the personal confidence of King Zwide and frequently visited him in his kraal where he got what information he wanted for Shaka and, in turn, falsely advised Zwide of Shaka's military dispositions. Then, when it suited Shaka best, Noluju informed Zwide that Shaka's forces were unprepared and vulnerable.

At the time of Qokli Hill, when the Zulu first clashed with the Ndwandwe, Shaka's survival can be ascribed largely to his plan to deprive the enemy of water, coupled with his brilliant tactical strategy.

Now, with the second conflict inevitable, Shaka again planned well ahead and carefully. Instead of thirst, he decided to confront the enemy warriors with a 'hungry earth'.

Shaka/Soshangane Battle

The Ndwandwe kingdom was up to the north in the Black Mfolozi area near Nongoma and Shaka's Zulu empire was to the south near Eshowe and the Mhlatuze River, not far from the dense and ancient Nkandla forest.

The Zulu leader knew that when they attacked him, the Ndwandwe would only be able to carry enough food to see them through the first few days and then they would have to sack the local kraals and take their grain and cattle for food. He planned with this in mind. He made all his people empty their grain pits and hide the contents in the forest or wherever else it could not easily be found, together with any other surplus food that they had. The Zulu kraals were, in this way, denuded and Shaka then similarly evacuated all the women and children and the aged to the cover of the forest and to other places of safety. Finally, he moved all the Zulu cattle out of the battle area with the exception of some, which he kept back to use as decoys to entice the Ndwandwe deeper into a 'wilderness' and further away from home.

In Ndwandweland, Zwide was excited by the false statements which Noluju whispered in his ear about the state of affairs at Shaka's kraal. He launched eighteen thousand prancing warriors on their journey southwards to silence, forever, the only threat of any importance to his complete domination of Nguniland – namely, Shaka and his Zulu. At the head of this Ndwandwe army stood the redoubtable Soshangane.

After two days of marching the Ndwandwe reached Zulu country, and having run out of rations they began to forage around for food but they found nothing; only deserted kraals with empty grain pits – where they expected a fight, they found no enemy. Shaka, meantime, kept his impi's or armies continuously out of sight and far ahead of the enemy, but he flaunted exciting targets of apparently straggling Zulu warriors just ahead of the Ndwandwe to lure them on. Strange to say, the Ndwandwe never managed to catch up with the stragglers, nor did they succeed in capturing any more of the decoy cattle left behind by Shaka as additional bait, than was intended to keep them advancing.

Shaka's trail led them on towards the mediaeval and impenetrable Nkandla Forest in a wild goose chase after a ghost army. Hunger gnawed at the stomachs of the Ndwandwe warriors; the circumstances were strange, the surroundings eerie and supernatural and, because most black people have an inherent fear of the unknown, they soon became superstitious and jittery.

In the meantime, Shaka hid his army in clearings in the forest with which he was familiar. One night, without realising their proximity to the Zulu, the Ndwandwe camped in a sheltered spot on the fringe of the forest. Shaka was delighted because, being the genius that he was, he knew that psychology in warfare could be as devastating as the brutal use of his stabbing spear. This was an opportunity he had planned and hoped for and Shaka never let a chance go by. In the dark eerie hours of that night when the chilling calls of jackals filled the air and the laugh of hyaenas (believed to be the tools of witches) seemed to aid and abet him, Shaka sent a silent, stealthy raiding party to do murder among the sleeping Ndwandwe. His men moved into the enemy camp with ghostly noiselessness and picked their victims. Man after man died before the uproar started.

The operation was so cunningly and mysteriously executed that the Ndwandwe were convinced that it was all supernatural and the work of witches. Pandemonium and terror broke loose and, in the confusion, Ndwandwe even killed Ndwandwe. Then as silently as they came, the Zulu melted back into the night and were gone. But no Ndwandwe warrior could sleep again that night and this, of course, was exactly what Shaka had planned – an enemy as tired as he was hungry and also stricken with fear of every known and unknown evil in this bedevilled forest.

Next morning, General Soshangane of the Ndwandwe decided to turn about face and head for home. When he reached open country, Shaka came out after him with his own excited warriors who had waited a long time for this moment. Like released springs they flew into Zwide's men, but with a plan. The Zulu tricked the enemy into opening their ranks in one or two places and then drove in wedges which took an ugly toll of lives before they pulled out again without wasting their own manpower unnecessarily in circumstances which were not yet exactly what Shaka wanted. He planned to throw everything into an open conflict and so gamble on all he had. This day was to be the last sunset for many brave men.

The Zulu followed the retreating enemy and harassed them at every opportunity like terriers biting at their heels. The territory was rugged and rough and still too tortuous for any form of organised battle. Shaka, however, was an opportunist and had the patience to wait his chance. This finally came as the Ndwandwe descended the hills now known as *Hlabizulu* – which in this context means 'the place of the Zulu stabbings' – and when they reached the flat basin of the Mhlatuze River below, Soshangane's Ndwandwe troops began to cross at a shallow drift a little upstream to the west of where the little Mvuzane River has its confluence with the bigger Mhlatuze. By strange coincidence, this crossing is only a few kilometres from the spot named 'Bulls Run' downstream from the confluence where Shaka was born.

The Zulu were heavily outnumbered but, with the Ndwandwe broken up at the crossing, Shaka sent his barefooted warriors racing down the hill at them.

HISTORY AND TRADITION

As head of his family line and a senior man in his neighbourhood the dignity of this Cele man exemplifies the respect he traditionally commands. He stands here in his cattle byre which women do not enter, other than in exceptional cases. It is sacred ground visited by the spirits of the family's ancestral fathers as far back as anyone can remember them and beyond.

49

The warrior King Shaka's highest personal award for gallantry was a hand-made necklace of wild-olive wood.

This ivory arm-band was said to have been worn by Shaka himself. Both this band and the award for valour are in the Killie Campbell Africana Museum, Pietermaritzburg.

The head of Shaka's own staff of office.

A high-ranking man of the Ntombela clan in his ceremonial dress. Traditionally, the leopard skin may only be worn by Chiefs and the King and any leopard killed is their property.

52   An historical picture by G.F. Angas of Zulu blacksmiths of old at work. (The Killie Campbell Africana Museum).

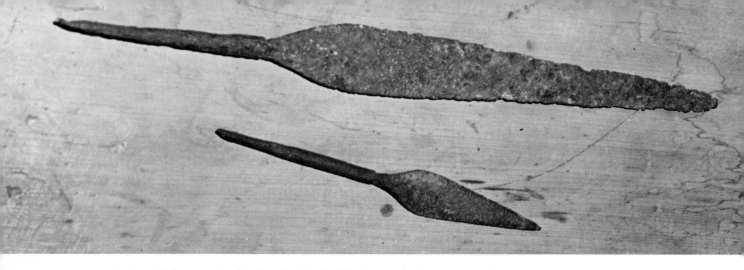

Ancient Zulu spearheads of probably the Shakan period.

The art of the blacksmith and metal-worker of old is almost completely extinct among the clansmen today but a few men still have some knowledge of it.

A proud family head.

Umname nephew of Chaka

A Zulu warrior of about 1840 at the end of Dingane's reign. This painting by G.F. Angas illustrates the size of the battle shields which were supposed to reach from a man's ankle to his chin. (The Killie Campbell Africana Museum).

Left: Paring the shaft of a new assegai.

Some Royal councillors at King Zwelithini's 'Great Place'.

A fine speciman of a man in his ceremonial regalia only about 50 kilometres from Durban.

Warriors in ceremonial dress in about 1840 as depicted by the artist G. F. Angas. (The Killie Campbell Africana Museum).

An artist's impression of King Cetshwayo whose warriors won a resounding victory at the Battle of Isandlwana in 1879, even though they ultimately lost the war to the British.

A Zulu spear and a British bullet case found on the battlefield of Isandlwana a century after the awe inspiring battle.

An artist's impression of the scene at Rorke's Drift on the morning of 23rd January 1879 after the all-night battle which won the Victoria Cross – Queen Victoria's highest award for valour – for *eleven* British Red-Coat soldiers.

Part of the Battlefield at Isandlwana as it is today.

An artist's impression of the scene at Isandlwana before the battle between Lord Chelmsford's forces and King Cetshwayo's Zulu warriors on the 22nd January 1879.

(Ack. The Killie Campbell Africana Museum for the use of the three drawings on these two pages).

63

Hangaza, of the Ntombela, on the left, was a wealth of information to me in my research. He discusses a point here with a friend.

They hit the enemy in the water from the rear. The fighting was violent and relentless and the river flowed red with blood. The battle swayed back and forth and then Shaka ran into trouble when the Ndwandwe rallied and hit back with deadly fury. The situation which Shaka saw from his vantage point on the hill behind was serious. His men were in grave danger and if they were not rescued immediately would be wiped out. Quick action was imperative.

The river ran through the battlefield from west to east and restricted movement on those two flanks, so that Shaka could not use his 'buffalo horns' tactics. The Ndwandwe, for their part, could either continue their retreat to the north while they fought a rearguard action at the drift or – and this was the danger to Shaka – they could stand and fight it out with the Zulu spearhead and probably annihilate them. Time was vital and Shaka knew it so he sent off post haste a contingent in an encircling move to his right (east) to cross the Mvuzane stream and then to swing left over the Mhlatuze, below the battle, and back westwards to come in on the Ndwandwe from their north which was their escape route. Shaka's lightning move caught the Ndwandwe unawares and they suddenly found themselves with Zulu to the north and Zulu to the south and with the river hampering their escape on the two flanks. King Zwide's army was trapped.

General Soshangane, quick to realise the futility of the situation, relinquished his grip and fled for his life to seek fame elsewhere on another day. Some of his followers managed to escape with him but many more, probably thousands, died that day in the battle of the Mhlatuze River.

Zwide himself was, of course, still safe and sound back at his royal kraal about one hundred kilometres north of the Mhlatuze valley, but Shaka wanted *him* in person. He picked a contingent of his fastest Zulu soldiers and ordered them to get to Zwide before any news of the battle could reach him. The warriors arrived at his kraal within twenty-four hours but Zwide, wily to the last, escaped and fled far to the north and out of Shaka's immediate reach.

Ntombazi of the Scalps

The Zulu contingent, hotly pursuing the fleeing remnants of the Ndwandwe forces, did however collect a major trophy for their leader in the form of Ntombazi, Zwide's mother, and in his own calculated time, Shaka despatched her in a manner so cruel that only he could have devised it.

As a price for her museum of scalps, she was condemned to die under the snapping jaws of a half-crazed, starving hyaena and so was shut up with it in a grass hut which was their joint prison. Ntombazi withstood the onslaught of the hyaena for two days and two terrifying nights but after parts of her legs had been torn off and savagely eaten by the hungry creature, she could stand it no longer and begged Shaka to be merciful and set the hut alight so that she could at least watch the animal die with her. Shaka conceded, and in an inferno of flames the grass 'beehive' collapsed in a blazing mass over the two*.

Zwide's Last Flurry

Terrified at the prospect of falling into Zulu hands, Zwide did not stop his headlong flight to safety until he had crossed both the Pongola and Komati Rivers and penetrated deep into Pedi (North Sotho) country to the west of Swaziland. Two sons and a number of fleeing clansmen joined him on his

*E. A. Ritter's *Shaka Zulu* gives a graphic description of these last hours of Ntombazi's existence.

65

journey and eventually they settled in the territory of the Pedi chief, Tulwana. Despite the fact that Zwide and his band were but the remnants of a once mighty army, they apparently retained a good measure of their former arrogance and strength and without much effort took control of the easygoing and inherently gentle Pedi people. However, this intrusion by a pretentious foreigner into the hitherto peaceful scene aroused deep resentment in the ample bosom of Tulwana's neighbour, the renowned Mjanji*, chieftainess of another group of Pedi people. Legend has it that this remarkable female was immortal and endowed with awesome supernatural powers. She could, for instance, make herself invisible at opportune moments and could summon plagues or pests at will and direct them against her enemies. In addition, she was physically set apart from all other females by being endowed with an extra pair of pendulous breasts which earned her the nickname of Queen 'Mabelemane' (Four-Breasts) by which she was known far and wide. Mjanji was determined to prevent Zwide from expanding his territorial claims in her direction, so she set her magic powers to work against him. Whether as a result of this or because of other more natural causes will never be known, but it is an established fact that soon after this King Zwide went into a decline and, despite the valiant efforts of his womenfolk and medicine men to keep him going, died after about five years in exile.

The History Makers Perhaps one of the most remarkable features related to the epic battle between the Ndwandwe and the Zulu in 1819, was the fact that amongst those fighting on that occasion were five of the most notable and intrepid trailblazers in the history of the black nations of Southern Africa. Each of whom left an inerasable influence on the lives of their people.

Firstly there was Shaka, towering over his Zulu and forging a new nation out of a clan. Then on the opposite side was Soshangane who, with a remnant of Zwide's vanquished army, eventually made his way northwards into Mozambique where he went on the rampage, finally to achieve fame as the founder of the Shangane nation whose kingdom stretched from north of Maputo (Lourenco Marques) to the banks of the Zambezi River. Alongside Shaka in the ranks of the Zulu was Mzilikazi who, in his turn, went rampaging through areas of the Transvaal, Orange Free State and Bechuanaland (now Botswana), gathering momentum as he went, to end up in Rhodesia where he built his Bulawayo kraal and founded the Matabele nation. Ultimately his territory stretched right up to Salisbury and beyond. Next there was Shaka's ultimate successor, his surly, brooding, jealous half-brother Dingane, who later murdered the Boer pioneer Piet Retief and his group of men. Then, perhaps least spectacular of the five was Mpande – Shaka's half-brother by yet another of old Senzangakona's many wives. Mpande eventually helped the Boers overthrow Dingane and himself took the Zulu throne to give them thirty years of peace and a great heir named Cetshwayo.

It was this same Cetshwayo's warriors who, sixty years later in 1879, made headlines which were blazoned around the world when they routed something like one thousand two hundred of Lord Chelmsford's British Red-Coats and

*It appears that the name Mjanji is not a personal name but was the name given to successive rulers of the Pedi people and for a number of generations these all appear to have been females. This would explain the perpetuation of the name and the theory of immortality ascribed to the four-breasted Mjanji of this period. According to A. T. Bryant she died in 1895.

allied forces in an hour and a half at the battle of Isandlwana in old Zululand, and silenced every gun before they raced on through rugged hills to Rorke's Drift, fourteen kilometres away, to engage the small British garrison defending the post there. This second battle too was an epic in history but less one-sided. Out of the small Red-Coat garrison which held the Zulu at bay for twelve hours that night, eleven of them won the Victoria Cross for their gallantry. Never before or since, has this been equalled in any single battle.

The Score Finally Settled

Old King Zwide far up north was succeeded by his son Sikunyana who was obsessed by an ambition for revenge on Shaka and also with the idea of leading his people back to their traditional homeland. By the middle of 1826 his plans and preparations for an invasion were complete. Shaka, for his part, was now at the peak of his power and equally determined to remove the hated Ndwandwe from the scene forever. When his spies informed him of Sikunyana's plans, he set out in characteristic fashion with his entire army and its entourage numbering in all some fifty thousand warriors and attendants, to meet the enemy half way. For days they marched in an endless column across the hot dusty plains of Northern Natal to where the enemy had already encamped on the slopes of a hill known as Ndololwane, in the area south-west of Piet Retief near where the village of Luneberg stands today.

Shaka halted his forces in the dense forests nearby and prepared for battle by inciting his men and whipping them up into a frenzy of hatred for the enemy and adulation of their king. After a day and a night he gave the order for attack and they swarmed up the slopes of Ndololwane, intent on annihilating the Ndwandwe. According to the historian, C. T. Binns, this was one of the most significant battles ever fought in the history of the Zulu nation. The hand-to-hand fighting was unbelievably fierce, the field was littered with corpses and within two hours the Ndwandwe were thrashed. They turned and fled with the triumphant Zulu warriors close on their heels.

Sikunyana and a few loyal supporters escaped death by hiding in a pit dug as an elephant trap. They then made their way to Swaziland and from there gained temporary sanctuary with Soshangane who was Sikunyana's relative and now was well-established as a ruler in his own domain. Thereafter, they moved on to new adventures elsewhere and finally left Shaka unchallenged, to reign supreme over his Zululand.

The Royal Lineage

Shaka never married, but it is said that he had a son by a girl in his enormous harem. It is also said that he immediately had the mother and child adopted by a tribe far to the south – suggested to be the Tembu of the Transkei – in case the child ever grew up to threaten his throne. However, nothing was ever heard of either of them again.

It is of interest to record that Shaka's blood line, the progeny of the sons of his father, Senzangakona, by several wives, can be traced unbroken right down to the existing reigning monarch Zwelithini Goodwill kaCyprian Bhekuzulu.

Chapter 3
The Valley of History

It was in this way then, that the Zulu nation was formed. Perhaps it would be more appropriate to say was 'forged' out of Shaka's broad-bladed spear – or assegai, as it is better known in South Africa.

The White Thread
Back in 1819 Shaka had not yet seen a white man. In fact as previously mentioned, he met his first in 1825. This was when Henry Francis Fynn and a small band of fellow soldiers-of-fortune came to visit him. They were British pioneers from the Cape of Good Hope and came to Natal as its first white settlers. They landed at Port Natal – now Durban – in two little ships in 1824 but Shaka refused to see them until the next year when sufficient time had elapsed to impress the newcomers with his importance by making them wait. In that time too, no doubt, he had them carefully watched to satisfy himself that they were not witches or workers in magic with plans to harm him.

The first of these ships was the *Julia*. It carried a small party led by Fynn. Then the *Anne* came six weeks later with Lieutenant Farewell in command. Both men left their names deeply engraved in the history of this new colony belonging to Great Britain. By 1835 a little mud village had grown up where the two ships landed and the place was called D'Urban after Sir Benjamin D'Urban, Governor of the Cape.

Shaka had no interest in Natal as part of his kingdom but ravaged and burned it and left it as a buffer 'no-man's-land' so that the Pondo and Xhosa tribes from the south beyond the Umzimkulu River, could not easily come through and make a surprise attack on him.

He almost exterminated the black tribes in Natal south of the Tugela and their few stray members who survived in hiding were left starving and some even became cannibals to stay alive.

After Fynn's arrival in 1824 many of these waifs and strays found shelter with him and they could have jeopardised his life, but Shaka was an unpredictable leader and not only condoned Fynn's action in sheltering them but, after a few years, made him chief of a group of them. They were called the Nkumbe (wanderers) and Chief Fynn made his headquarters to the south of Durban, near the Umzumbi River, not far from the present Port Shepstone. I think it is interesting to mention here that Fynn's younger brother Frank, who subsequently joined him, is buried in this area at Paddock. Frank's death was not without drama. He died while Henry was away and their loyal Zulu friends buried him according to their own tradition, together with his 'favourite possessions'. Among these was big brother Henry's diary of his first three years in Natal. This diary was invaluable as history and some of it had been laboriously written at times with ink made from crushed flowers. On his return to Natal, Henry dared not dig up his brother's remains because only witches or *mthakathi* tamper with graves and everyone of his Zulu would have deserted him had he done so.

Shaka liked Fynn and in his far-sightedness instantly saw the potential in him. He told his people that Fynn and the other few white men who had come with him had knowledge and intelligence far ahead of theirs and that they must *learn* from them and take advantage of their presence. He threatened with death any Zulu who hurt them.

Fynn became a regular visitor to Shaka's royal kraal and took him trinkets and trappings and – perhaps even more appreciated – simple medicines like purgatives. These latter were particularly exciting because 'cleansing' is an important part of Zulu rituals and Fynn's medicines, even though simple, were potent.

Natal in 1824 was rugged in the extreme and completely wild but Fynn was a man of courage and determination and had powers of endurance which saw him through many a crisis. In due course, when his clothes wore out, he roamed Natal barefooted dressed in tatters and in skins. Basically he was an elephant hunter and a trader, but he was not a natural writer. Nevertheless, to his credit, he knew he was in the midst of history and was determined to preserve what he could of it for posterity. He rewrote the first three years of his lost diary as best he could from memory and with endless patience, then kept it up to date. Wherever he went after that the diary, carried on a porter's head, went with him, wrapped in an elephant's ear to protect it from the weather. Thanks is due to Fynn for much of what we know of the early Zulu and of those transitionary years in Natal when they first came into contact with the white people of the south.

Role of the White Traders

As a trader, Fynn started a new way of life by bringing to the Zulu fragments of civilisation from the outside world. After Fynn other white traders followed in his footsteps and became increasingly important in the life of the people of the kraals. So much so that today they are a vital part of the tribesmen's way of life, particularly in some of the remote areas of their homeland. The traders buy the Zulu's surplus corn, hides and skins, and in turn sell them sugar and salt and basic luxuries like condensed milk and gaily-coloured cloths and beads. Another line which is sold, mostly to the girls, is sparkling white sand-shoes – or tackies ('teckies') as they call them. These are the ultimate in fashion and together with rolled up black umbrellas are a 'must' for any well-dressed girl. To me however, they are a jarring note, and foreign in a girl's attractive regalia of massed beads of all colours on her bare-breasted ebony-like body. Furthermore, shoes are seldom worn with the intention of protecting the feet, because the Zulu of the kraals go barefooted from childhood and are used to the rough pathways.

In my travels in Zulu country I have often stayed with white traders in their warm and hospitable homes. I will always treasure the friendships I have made there. Their sincerity is something which seems to have grown out of their contact with the simple country tribesmen and women. They have absorbed the principles of people who live close to nature and who have learned to help each other and to share. The Zulu mind is unpolluted by selfishness and the traders reflect this characteristic in their own attitudes to their fellow men and, not least, to the Zulu. The tribesman, for his part, develops a great affinity and loyalty towards the trader and regards him as his 'father' and benefactor. Most of the old-timers would rather die protecting such a white friend than harm him.

69

To some extent the Zulu country folk take certain things for granted, but they are the things which they themselves would automatically do for the next man without thinking of them as favours or of being worthy of comment.

An example of this is seen right back in childhood where all the little girls act as nursemaids and help any mother, whether family or not, who has her hands full. At the end of the day when the mother takes her baby over again, the little voluntary nursemaid goes scampering happily back to her playmates without thought of reward or thanks.

Most city dwellers will have seen how, when someone's car stalls in the street, half a dozen black passers-by rush to push it. Then, the moment it starts they run cheerfully off on their own business laughing and joking without even looking back for a word of praise. It is just in their nature to help in everyday things, but if in turn some special favour or exceptional kindness is shown them like the giving of a gift to one of their children, they are warm and profound in their gratitude. In fact, it is a custom among the Zulu for any friend standing by to add *his* thanks to that of the recipient of a gift. I have often experienced this when I have perhaps given a few cents to a cripple by the wayside. Not only the cripple has thanked me, but any other Zulu passing by has also added his 'We praise you!' They do not have a direct equivalent of 'thank you' but say, 'We praise you – *Siyabonga!*'

This then, is the Zulu. The trader in his turn is a 'father' to the simple kraal folk around him. They bring their problems to him; he helps them in a drought and he gives their children medicine. As a result there is a touching, warm, understanding between the two.

Some of the moments I enjoy most in my travels are those at the end of a day's research or photography when I sit in the evening with a trader and his wife on their lawn beside a barbecue fire. We exchange stories of experiences and talk about Zulu customs and rituals and history. Then we go to bed, hours later, with every door and window in the house wide open and listen to the sounds of the night-jar, a distant drum or a cow lowing. It is the music of the Zulu wilds.

I must in fairness admit that there can be experiences in this kind of life which are not so pleasant. One I had was in the middle of a dark night when an inquisitive horse came into my room and snorted loudly into my sleeping face.

Life Today in the Valley of History

The Natal and KwaZulu white people are keenly interested in Zulu culture and history. Most of those living in the rural areas speak the Zulu language and so do many townsmen. The benefit of this cannot be overrated because it is surely the best possible way to understand the tribesmen.

One evening at the home of my trader friends Kingsley and Jill Holgate, near Eshowe, the story came up of Shaka Zulu's second victory over Zwide and his Ndwandwe army. The scene of this battle on the Mhlatuze River is not far from their home and so Kingsley and I decided to visit it. It is a place relatively few white people have seen because of its inaccessibility. The hills and valleys in the area are so rugged that the battleground can only be reached on foot in at least a day's hike or partly by a four-wheel drive and then on foot. The Mhlatuze in the area is the home of crocodiles, and in addition its bush-covered banks and the hills around shelter the odd leopard and black mamba snakes. We decided to take a vehicle even though it meant covering a longer distance.

The battle area is towards the Nkandla forest from Eshowe and is a little west of the confluence of the Mvuzane and Mhlatuze Rivers. The territory, in general, is not only important because of Shaka's victory there – which consolidated the supremacy of the Zulu – but because Shaka was born only about ten kilometres from the battlescene at a place now called 'Bull's Run' just to the east of the confluence. Both spots will disappear under the waters of the Mhlatuze River and be lost to history in the 1980's when a dam wall is completed across the river to provide water for the town of Richard's Bay.

South Africa, including the land of the Zulu, is so often referred to as a 'land of contrasts' that I am hesitant to use the phrase again, but the day I went into the Mhlatuze valley I went into what seemed to be another world – yesterday's world. My years of research would have been the poorer without this experience.

The pattern of life in the valley is old and traditional; the huts are true Zulu 'beehive' and their arrangement in the kraal shows roughly how many wives each family head has. I was surprised to see that numbers of them have up to six. The impact of this and, for that matter, even of single wife marriages on population growth can be imagined when it is considered that tribespeople are not exponents of birth control in married life and that they regard large families as a blessing of the Creator. I once came across a man in the Tugela River valley who has sixteen wives and sixty-six children. He is a successful diviner (witch-doctor) and much respected.

Among the Zulu, wives are synonomous with wealth because a man pays an average of eleven head of cattle for his bride in *lobolo* (dowry) and his ability to acquire many wives proves his success in life. They are his status symbol.

In the valley we found the place called 'Bulls Run' where Shaka was born. From here we gazed up at the Hlabizulu hills where thirty-two years later in 1819 Shaka led his troops down into the Mhlatuze drift below to victory over his arch enemies, the Ndwandwe, to emerge as founder and first king of a new Zululand.

The scene where all this happened left me in awe. These hills are so rugged and overgrown that it seems unbelievable that there were men who had the stamina and the strength and the agility to fight hand-to-hand with spears in such a place. But then Shaka never looked for the easiest way in anything he did, but rather the most effective.

Because of its inaccessibility this valley of decision has still scarcely been touched by civilisation and it remains one of the most primitive regions of today's KwaZulu. In it the way of life of the people is probably still very close in many ways to what it must have been nearly two centuries ago.

This valley fascinates me because it is unspoiled and the people in it remain largely unsophisticated, simple and honest. They have not been confused by the hustle of modern living and their laws are those that nature and necessity taught them. Here a man still shares himself with his neighbour as part of a law of survival.

I was reminded in the valley of many other moments that are still treasures in my memory – quiet chats in the shade of a tree with some old veteran about the magic and myth and the protocol and etiquette which keeps life in the kraals almost as if in a cocoon.

Traditions of the Kraal

When Kingsley Holgate and I went into the valley, our mutual friend and artist Beryl Wood came with us. The scene as we reached the escarpment left her breathless as it did each of us.

On the escarpment, running westwards of Eshowe, are lush green fields of sugar-cane and we emerged suddenly from these to find ourselves looking over a vast basin patterned with deep valleys and great hills. The scene stretched away and was lost in the distance. The sun had passed its zenith and shone towards us to put each prominence into silhouette. It painted the hazes in the valleys between in purples and pinks and blues according to their distance from us.

The 'road' immediately ahead was less attractive and even our otherwise detailed area map showed us little that helped. Fortunately it is never necessary to stop long in KwaZulu before someone comes along who always knows something about the area, or who knows someone else nearby who does.

Our man came from the Ntuli clan and, Zulu-like, politely asked what was wrong. He told us he lived down in the 'first' valley and he looked with interest at the empty space in the rear of our small truck. He would be happy to show us the way as far as he could. Then, he saw someone else approaching us leading a rather reluctant goat and said 'Hawu! Yes . . . this man knows those deeper parts well!' Before we could comment he called out to him: '*Wena, Langeni, sondela*' (you, Langeni, come nearer). Langeni came and he did know where 'Bulls Lun'* was. In fact, he lived near there. He said: 'It is where the Zulu long ago hammered the Ndwandwe!'

He was on his way to his home which was near there. He – with his goat – was most willing to guide us and without further ado hastily joined Ntuli who had already secured his place on the back of our vehicle. We started on our way with the four-wheel drive in its lowest gear. There was a roadway of sorts through the scrubby bush with stones in it half as high as the wheels and potholes half as deep. We progressed sometimes at three kilometres an hour, sometimes at two and occasionally at ten. But every moment was exciting. Ntuli and Langeni soon learned what interested us and each time we stopped pointed out places where 'incidents' had happened in the Zulu battle. They repeatedly drew our attention to some or other aspect of the historical Hlabizulu range of hills.

At one stop I asked Langeni about his goat which was obviously going to be sacrificed to his ancestors. He said he had paid thirty-five Rand for it (it was hardly three-quarters grown). When I asked him how he had planned to get it home in the heat of the valley in such rough country, he stood up and straddled it and showed me how he would have stopped it from falling over when it became tired. He said that when it lay down from exhaustion he would have carried it to the nearest kraal and left it there to rest for the night.

I asked him: '*le' Mbuzi inhlatshelwe-ni?*' (This goat, it is stabbed for what?)

'*Amadlozi*' (the ancestral spirits), he replied.

I asked him more about it and he said his father's ancestors 'are hungry for meat and if we don't give it to them, they will punish us with bad crops. They don't like us to neglect them'.

As we went back to the vehicle Kingsley said: 'Where could you find greater loyalty? Imagine dragging that poor creature through all this for two days! It makes you realise how intense their religion is and to what lengths they will go in practising it.'

As we penetrated deeper into the valley, so we found the homes to be more traditional and nearly all were of the old 'beehive' style. It was delightful to see

*The unschooled Zulu cannot pronounce an 'r' as an equivalent consonant does not exist in his language.

numbers of kraals laid out in the old orthodox pattern in a circle. The hut of the head of the family is always in the most prominent spot possible on the highest ground, overlooking the huts of his wives. More specific details of the layout of such a kraal will be given later in this book. It is very much as Shaka knew the scene and when I saw it I had the nostalgic feeling that I was living in history.

Much western clothing has unfortunately found its way into this area, as it has in most tribal areas, but we were fortunate in that our trip co-incided with a day when there was a tribal ceremony on and so numerous locals were dressed in their best Zulu beadwork and other forms of national finery. We became aware of the gathering crowds when we found ourselves passing numbers of bare-breasted girls going our way, carrying clay beer pots on their heads. The deportment of those with the better figures was elegance personified.

Zulu custom is that, for most ceremonies, the host supplies the meat – a goat or ox or whatever he can afford – and a measure of sorghum beer. The guests bring additional beer. It is usual for parties to go on for twenty-four hours or more until all the meat is eaten and the beer drunk. Guests start arriving around midday on the day the ox is killed – usually a Saturday – and the feasting and dancing and jollification goes on from there all through the night into the next day, at the end of which the guests start staggering home and sometimes fall down by the wayside to sleep.

And so our jaunt continued at a snail's pace as we lumbered over the heavy track. Then we began to hear a growing commotion from somewhere ahead of us. It came from dozens of noisy, boisterous voices. My heart skipped a beat because a commotion in a black gathering can mean danger. While everyone is cheerful everything is fine, but if someone is insulted or gets hurt, ugly trouble can erupt. Our road began to turn slowly to the right and the scrub began to clear into an opening on the left. At that moment a Zulu man came running out towards us, brandishing a stick. In his excitement his apron of fur tassels swung around somewhat indiscreetly. A few yards from us he threw up his arms to stop us and two rows of great white teeth flashed in a *welcoming* smile. He called out: 'Hawu! My chiefs! My chiefs! Come, we are *drinking* – it's a big occasion. Come!' My heartbeat settled back to normal and our artist friend, Beryl, visibly relaxed in her seat.

Beyond the man many people were squatting on the ground around a few pots of beer. We were told they had stopped to take some weight off the carrier-girls' heads! The pots, the man said, 'are very heavy in this sun!' Their kind deed had obviously refreshed the crowd judging by the loud and noisy welcome they gave us.

According to Zulu etiquette, guests cannot be allowed to go without a drink of beer when the host has beer available and we were soon offered ours. It came in a beer scoop made from a calabash (gourd) with a long neck and a side cut out so that it looked like a ladle. Had we been at a kraal, the utensil would have been a clay pot, but as travellers our hosts were not carrying their conventional drinking pots. Kingsley played his part with complete aplomb and drank the thin, pink, porridge-like brew with proper ceremony. Then with an appreciative 'Ahhh!' wiped his mouth with the back of his hand! Then, Zulu fashion, he stretched and put his flat hand on his stomach as a sign of satisfaction. My turn came next and I am not particularly partial to beer. I still have to forgive Beryl for a loud: 'Come on, Aubrey, you can do a lot better than that!'

It is bad manners among the Zulu to hurry away after a cursory greeting or a draft of beer, so we parleyed on about the absence of rain and how the cattle were getting thin as a result of this. Meanwhile dozens of little children from all around came to stand and stare at us. It was then that I saw something I have seldom seen. A little boy of about ten sidled up to an old man and stood close to him, as if in expectation. The old man ignored him until it was dignified to notice and then, from an old pouch, took a little crushed-up home-grown tobacco and gave it to him. The small one was waiting with a bit of grubby brown paper he had found lying around. He tore it into a square, licked the one edge heavily and with obvious experience rolled the tobacco into a cigarette. He then lit it, had a puff more than necessary and passed it up to the old man before he went skipping away to join his friends.

The Zulu are not heavy smokers like the Xhosa* and normally their women-folk do not smoke at all. Among the men, dagga or wild hemp has been smoked since their earliest days. Snuff is particularly popular with both sexes and a big proportion of it is home-made by mixing powdered kraal-grown tobacco with dry aloe leaves.

In the valley we enquired the reason for the celebration and one of the men assumed an air of great dignity and said: 'Hawu! it's a big occasion today! They killed an ox this morning over there.' He pointed down the valley then paused deliberately to let it sink in. 'Truly its a big thing. That man has many cattle . . . yes, he's got many cattle!'

I interpreted the clues and took a chance: 'Hawu! Then its his eldest daughter. She must be coming out today. It's her *cece* ceremony.'

He started in surprise: 'Yuh! How'd you know that?'

'I know because such a father has to share his happiness and give his friends meat! And he also has to boast a little so that everyone sees his wealth by the cattle he kills for feasts. Isn't that so?'.

'Hi! *Baba* (father) you speak the truth. I see you know our ways!' He would have loved to parley on, but we had places and things to see.

While we were talking Beryl watched the pottery going past balanced on the heads of girl porters. She was very excited and decided she *had* to acquire a pot for herself as a souvenir. But she knew that nothing would persuade any of these people to part with anything relative to a feast, because it would be inviting the displeasure of the ancestral spirits and so she anticipated our host's advice to try for one *after* we were out of the ritual zone. We were also aware of the futility of attempting any form of business on the day of the ceremony, firstly because tribespeople are too preoccupied then and secondly because it is dangerous to venture into anything that can cause a difference of opinion – like the price of a pot – when they have consumed a few litres of beer.

We promised Beryl to try for her trophy at a kraal out of the party-zone on our way home. So in the meantime we continued along our rugged track, deeper and deeper into the valley, stopping at intervals to revel in seeing kraal scenes which were like fragments out of history. To the uninitiated, no doubt, many of them would have been just another group of huts. But they were in orthodox Zulu pattern and what excited us, was 'reading' them.

By counting the number of huts in the kraal we could tell roughly how many wives were in it, or how good a farmer the head was by counting the number of maize storage huts in evidence.

*See *The Magic World of the Xhosa* – Aubrey Elliott

His wealth was determined by the size of his byre, and the degree to which he disciplined his wives by the state of orderliness of his establishment.

By this time we had dropped our Ntuli guide at his kraal, but Langeni and his goat were still with us and we marvelled continuously at the patience he would have needed to get it home to the sacrificial fire through this rugged area on foot.

Occasionally we reached a clearing where it would have been possible to turn the landcruiser to go back, but Langeni always forestalled any such ideas with: 'The road ahead is still good. We can get much further in this motor'. He had no intention of losing his lift so easily.

In due course we passed the kraal where the 'coming-out' ceremony was to be held. Excitement there was building up conspicuously, but it was obvious that the girls were still at the river washing. This is an important ritual with as much of a spiritual connotation as a physical one. It is a symbolic purification from 'uncleanness' of the girl who 'comes out' into the world as a debutante and part of her ritual is to spend the entire morning at the water washing with the girls of her retinue.

We went on into the low basin of the Mhlatuze and Mvuzane Rivers near their confluence. There we saw 'Bull's Run' where Shaka was born on the north bank of the Mhlatuze. A deserted old trading store now stands on the site with its roof rusting and its windows broken. Just upstream from here, the Mvuzane runs into the Mhlatuze and a short distance still further upstream in the Mhlatuze is the drift where the second and decisive Zulu/Ndwandwe battle took place which made Shaka the supreme leader of all the clans of what later became Zululand.

We left the Mhlatuze and swung left to come down on the Mvuzane, probably less than two kilometres up from the confluence. Its waters were cool and inviting. Not a big river, but it ran strongly for the dry season. Langeni got off here and said in Zulu:

'My Chiefs, now the "motor" can go no further. Its road ends here. I praise you; you have helped me. *Ngiyabonga!*'

He could not speak English or anything other than his own tongue so we wished him well for the rest of the journey with '*Hamba kahle*' (go well). We added, too, that we were sure that his ancestors were going to be happy with him for remembering them. This impressed him and he thought it would be very good if he and I and the goat had our photograph taken as he waded across the river. Before he disappeared on the far side of the river he waved another farewell.

It was cool beside the water, and as we wandered along the river banks we found a bird trap that little boys had made from reeds stuck into the sand and it brought back nostalgic memories to my mind of the days when I, too, was a little boy and made these same traps with my Xhosa childhood friends on my father's sheep farm nearly nine hundred kilometres to the south, in the Eastern Cape. The Xhosa are basically blood brothers of the Zulu in that they both come from Nguni origin*.

The only way out of the valley was back along the same track by which we had come. This meant passing the ceremonial kraal again, where by this time they had been drinking for two hours. I felt a trace of apprehension about this

*See *The Magic World of the Xhosa*

75

because there was no certainty as to what sort of mood they would be in. While beer-drinks invariably start off in spirits of cheer and goodwill, any minor incident like an insult thrown somewhere among the women, can start a conflagration with assegais and knobkerries. Then skulls get cracked, blood flows and frequently people are killed. In these incidents women usually figure prominently by taking sides and inciting their menfolk, but often a strong man – frequently the host himself – strides into the midst of the trouble and lashes the culprits with a verbal tirade, or he might even take up a stick and silence them with a few cracking blows.

The tribespeople, of course, respect strength as much as they despise weakness. Discipline to them is a way of life and they will die for a courageous *leader* who shows them the way. On the other hand they are often slow to act *individually* in extra-ordinary circumstances.

Etiquette

As we got nearer the party area we passed numbers of young men and teenage girls on their way to the beer drink, and I became worried because not one of them greeted us. They looked right through us and beyond us as if we were not there. My mind went back to Xhosa people to the south who wave and call out cheerful greetings to every passing white man they see. I was confused and my mind began to search – was this antagonism? As I wondered it occurred to me that we were in one of the most primitive parts of KwaZulu and one of the most tradition-orientated. I thought, in particular, of their laws of respect which also include their form of greeting. Then I realised that we might be at fault in not greeting them first. So when we came to the next group, I raised my hand and said with a smile: 'Sawubona!' (I see you) The reaction was spontaneous. Everyone smiled and came back with 'Sanibona Mnumzana!' (We see you, Sir) I literally felt myself relax and I realised how tense I had been, but such moments are not new to me.

The principle involved in this old Zulu custom of greeting is a simple and a logical one. It arises from the fact that boys and girls have very little status in kraal life and must show respect to their seniors in all they do. They are taught that until they reach adult status they are 'little' (unimportant) people and it would be presumptuous of them to greet a senior first because the senior might not even have 'seen them' and 'not want to see' them as it would be below his dignity. Once a junior's existence has been acknowledged by his senior, however, then he may greet with proper courtesy, even with excitement, because he has been seen by one so important.

This was my experience in this particular area, but I have found in practice that local environmental influence often changes customs like this, and in many regions the junior *does* greet the senior first, because the senior is insulted if he is ignored!

Protocol in the kraal is strict and complex and the more I experience it the more impressed I am with the dignity it breeds. It is a culture founded on respect; the respect of a son for his father, the father for his chief and the chief for his king. Beyond this it is a society of patriarchs where the women are subservient to their men and again pay respect to them in many ways prescribed by tradition.

One of the most poignant occasions I have experienced exhibiting the respect the Zulu pay to their superiors, was on a day at the Zulu King's own 'Great Place' or royal house near Nongoma. It began as I stood talking to a prince of the royal lineage in the courtyard. A man arrived with a message for the prince and he immediately went down on his knees in front of him, clasped the royal hand in both of his and said his words while looking up to the prince's face in awestruck reverence. The prince gave him an order with splended dignity and the messenger rose and walked away backwards in a stooped posture for a good long distance until he ultimately turned his back towards us and hurried away. A few minutes later King Goodwill himself arrived and took me to see his personal household warriors or guards, whose barracks of beehive grass huts adjoin his grounds. As we came into view every man in sight leapt to his feet, raised his right hand and roared a thundering salute of 'Bayede!' Each time we came into sight again, no matter if we had only been around a hut, the king was given a repeat of the royal salute. Each time he responded with a calm, admirable grace until eventually when we were well out of sight and away from any man's presence, he was able to relax completely.

King Zwelithini Goodwill KaCyprian Bhekuzulu is a direct descendant of the first man Zulu and is the sixteenth ruler to head his dynasty which dates back to Malandela, Zulu's father, and the founder of the family line. This assumes that early legend is accurate and it includes the ill-fated Sigujana who ruled briefly prior to Shaka.

But I have deviated from the feast in the valley where a century and a half ago, these same people were consolidated into one nation by their remarkable leader, Shaka.

The track we were on passes within a few metres of the host kraal on its right and, as we came into sight of the kraal over a rise, there was a gasp from each of us in the cab. There were hundreds of people everywhere. The entire track ahead was blocked with dancing, singing, milling people. Bare-breasted girls sang and danced and shouted noisily, encouraged by teenage boys who did mock-battle with knobkerries and shields. Men sat around drinking and women brought on their beer.

We came forward slowly and our vehicle edged into the scattered people on the fringe of the crowd. It began to nose at a snail's pace deeper into the throng. It was risky because had we bumped or hurt anyone, we would have been mobbed. People in our direct path edged sideways to let us in but they were so engrossed in the main scene of the day which was on our left, that they were hardly conscious of our presence.

| 'Coming-out' or Cece Ceremony for Girls | In an arena, the girl whose 'coming-out' it was, danced with her troupe of thirty or forty girls. She wore a leather skirt or *sidwaba* and the lace-like caul of fat which comes from the inside of an ox which had been killed for her. Her head was through the middle of the sheet which had stretched to about fifty-five centimetres square (twenty inches) and draped itself over her naked breasts in the front and down her back. It had been pliable when she put it on but now it had hardened into something like a sheet of armour. |

In the centre of the crowd we stopped because it would have been a breach of etiquette to go past without paying our respects first to the head of the family. We also hoped to see something of the *cece* ritual itself, but realised it would be bad manners to barge in on the scene without the host's consent, because a Zulu's home is his kingdom. He will welcome a sincere guest, but no-one dare intrude into his precincts without his goodwill and without the risk of his displeasure. We asked a messenger to announce our arrival.

The family head sat with a group of his fellow elders in a row watching the dancers. We saw him receive our message, but he neither turned nor showed any visible interest. I expected this, because if he had betrayed any nervous excitement it would have been a suggestion in Zulu eyes, of his personal inferiority. His dignity was at stake because a Zulu man must conduct himself as the *master* in his own home at all times. In due course, however, he did stand up and then graciously excused himself from his company and came over to us.

He knew of my trader friend, Kingsley Holgate, because the Zulu know their neighbours for long distances around. He gave him a warm welcome. Kingsley as before was faultless in his protocol and greeted the man with proper respect and praised him for the esteem in which the people held him as evidenced by their numbers present and by the quantity of beer there was. The Zulu was pleased and had difficulty in hiding the fact and said we could watch the ceremony for as long as we wished. With the need for the initial formality dispensed with, he became casual and at ease and with my friend he went down into the warrior's crouching position on his haunches for a chat on local affairs.

In keeping with Zulu etiquette beer was brought to us by his senior wife. She kneeled in front of her husband with a twelve-litre drinking pot in her hands and took a sip herself to prove it was not poisoned before she passed it to him. He, in turn, also had a sip before he passed it to his guest who, after a taste, put it on the ground where it was available to them both. By this time I was a little distance away taking photographs and so was brought my own beer. In a short while the merriment of the crowd grew to a pitch where we knew that any trivial incident among them could start an argument, so at an opportune moment we bade farewell to a chorus of '*Hamba-kahle!*' (go well) and went on our way.

Token Beer Drinks   We did not see adult life again for several kilometres. The kraals were empty except for small children and their nursemaids. In Zulu society parties are for everyone and specific invitations are not necessary. Everyone who lives near enough joins in. If there is anyone who is too old or too feeble to walk the distance, they celebrate by themselves at home – just to show 'how happy they are' for the other person!

I experienced an amusing incident of this kind on another occasion. It was on a hot afternoon about sunset as I made my way on foot back from a ceremony I had been to see. Thorn bushes and scraggy shrubs tore at my arms and my legs below my shorts, and I was busy thinking of black mamba snakes and scorpions when a shrill old woman's voice startled me from only a metre or two away. There she was, beside the path – an old, old granny, whom I knew. She tried to rise to give me the welcome she wished, but in the attempt keeled over sideways. She struggled to get up on her hands and knees. Then she giggled and looked up at me in what must have seemed a blurred haze above her. Her old eyes were obviously playing tricks and she laughed foolishly: '*Hawu! Baba* (Father)' she said. 'This is a great beer drink – a happy one. I waited to greet you here and now I have seen you I must get back home. Its a long way in the dark and I'll kick my toes against the stones when I walk.' I wondered how I could help her and then I heard children's voices and looked up to see the children themselves scampering down from old granny's kraal, not a hundred paces away.

I left her, busy scolding the little ones for bothering her 'big chief' (me) with their requests for 'Zweets'!

Material for Witches   On the last lap of our return journey out of the Mhlatuze valley, we came to a kraal where our trader-host knew its head and decided this would be a good place to try for the beer pot which Beryl Wood, our artist friend, wanted.

The Zulu greeted him warmly and after the softening-up niceties our host turned the conversation in the appropriate direction. Kingsley explained how he was showing us – his two guests – the country of the Zulu and how we were interested in their ways and how the 'chieftainess' wanted a clay pot to show her friends back home so she could boast about her journey into *his* land.

The Zulu looked at Kingsley, who has a great heavy beard, and laughed and turned to me.

'It's a good man who has a beard like that' he said. 'He will never bewitch anyone. He looks like a church minister!' His statement was poignant and implied that he was satisfied we had no evil intentions. This was in our favour because a Zulu will not easily let anything personal leave his family's possession in case it falls into the hands of a witch who might scrape dirt or other parts from it to use in magic medicine against the family.

The man called out to his youngest wife to bring 'such and such' a *khamba* (beer-pot) from his hut for the white lady. Beryl was delighted and a few days later became a conspicuous passenger on her plane bound for home, with a large Zulu beer-pot as part of her hand luggage.

Search for Artifacts   We continued our search for Zulu artifacts at the next kraal but as I expected, the going was not as easy because the family did not know us as in the previous case. We saw a man hewing a milk pail out of a log when we arrived and I decided that if he was making a *new* bucket he must be discarding an old one – probably an antique. But he dismissed any suggestion that he had another and I made no impression on him with my suggestion of an attractive price. He remained poker-faced. Of course I had no idea whether he really did have a discarded pail or not, but I was bent on a gamble so I called in the 'bearded minister' and he crouched in his friendly fashion beside the man and drew him into a chat about the weather and his crops and his cattle. Then, ultimately, in true Zulu fashion the man of the kraal came around to the subject of our health and our affairs. It was what Kingsley was waiting for. Patiently, and in careful detail, he explained where we came from, that we were interested in the culture and customs of the Zulu and that I was writing all about them for people in other places to read – just as I had done in the case of the Xhosa. This relaxed him and I think got him hoping that *his* picture might be in the book. In fact I expected him to ask me there and then to photograph him because there are few things which the Zulu love more than pictures of themselves.

His whole attitude changed, and just as if he had thought up a bright idea himself, he sent a little boy scurrying off to bring 'that old milk pail behind the byre'. A moment later another boy arrived with a second pail from somewhere else. Then the womenfolk came to join in the fun. The pails were weathered and cracked, but rare gems because although such things are still sometimes laboriously hand made by the old craftsmen, their place is gradually being taken by galvanised buckets bought from the local trading store. Before we left someone even brought two wooden sleeping pillows for my collection. These would have been a particularly valuable acquisition to a witch because they had years of head grease on them which could have been used for magic medicine. However, the kraal people had satisfied themselves that we had no evil intentions. In fact, one of the young wives set up a peal of laughter when she said '*Hawu!* The white people are funny. They pay real money for old pails that are cracked and can't even hold milk. What *good* are they?'

It was on that friendly note which has so often exhilarated my research travels that I came back from yesterday's world into civilisation. It was another of the times when I felt a little sad at the thought that the Zulu – with their own way of life – are leaving so much behind as they hurry out of their old world where nature is their parent and guide and guardian, into a confused new world where values and demands are so different. For a long time there will be much in the outside world that they will not understand or know adequately how to handle.

A MAN, HIS CHIEF AND THEIR KING

A man of high rank at King Zwelithini's 'Great Place'. He stands in the gateway of the King's cattle byre which is a particularly sacred place in the eyes of the Zulu people of the kraals.

A segment of the crowd which attended the formal installation by the South African Government of Zwelithini Goodwill Kacyprian Bkekuzulu as Paramount Chief of the Zulu on 3rd December 1971.

82

Cowhide back aprons and tasseled front aprons is normal dress for a traditionalist tribesman.

84   In spite of the beauty of some of their own beaded outfits, both males and females can seldom resist donning some or other item of western dress which appeals to them.

A beautifully dressed young family-head at a ceremony at his home kraal.

An important and impressive guest at the tribal ceremony of Zwelithini Goodwill's installation as king.

Chief Gatsha Buthelezi, Chief Executive Officer or Prime Minister, on the occasion of the King's installation on the 3rd January 1971.

Councillors at the King's royal establishment.

Married women of the Usutu clan at Nongoma.

Three of the nine wives of a diviner (witch-doctor) of the Cele clan. Except for minor items, all these wives dress in identical fashion whenever they go out.

No matter their importance, status or age, Zulu men can never resist a little fun with their sticks and shields when the opportunity arises.

92 Beads have been popular among the Zulu and most of South Africa's tribal peoples for generations and they use them in profusion; but their cost is now becoming almost prohibitive and in the foreseeable future they will probably disappear from the scene forever as a major fashion.

The necklace of the young man here has a duiker horn as a pendant. It is the conventional present a
young girl gives her boy-friend when they become engaged. The horn is usually filled with a
love-potion.

93

The King at his formal installation by the South African Government on the day preceding that of his own people. The lion and the elephant on his throne (*Ngonyama* and *Ndlovu*) are symbolic of power and strength – characteristics always associated by the Zulu with their king. The leopard skin is the dress of royalty.

Left: The Zulu King at his installation, on the 4th January 1971, by his own people following traditional customs.

96   A Zulu man dances (*jabulas*) when he wishes to express joy, excitement or appreciation.

Chapter 4
Structure of the Society

In KwaZulu life in the kraals follows almost a standard pattern. It is a pattern which is based on many of the old customs of Shaka's day and of long, long, before that.

The people, of course, are ancestor worshippers and in their behaviour they have largely to follow the dictates of the spirits of their forefathers. These requirements are highly complex and are made even more so by the interference of witches with their magic and medicine and by many other supernatural forces.

This is a very exciting aspect of their life but I cannot allow myself to dwell on it here. Sufficient for this book will be the telling of the tale of the day to day life of the Zulu of the kraals.

The word 'kraal' is the long established name for the homes of the country tribespeople of Southern Africa and it is not used only in respect of the Zulu. It is a word which is used broadly and may mean the single hut of a newly married couple, the larger establishment of a many-wived man or it may even be used to indicate a tribal village and also a byre.

The Hierarchy

The rural tribesman is basically a child of nature, the product of many generations of simple, illiterate folk whose lives are nevertheless governed by strict codes of honour and rules of etiquette. They have a deep-rooted respect for their elders and superiors which is truly admirable. These laws which dictate the pattern of their lives are splendid examples of how nature looks after her own – by teaching them the wisest ways to maintain an orderly society and to protect themselves in their journey through life. She has adapted them through the generations to derive maximum benefit for all from her gifts, borne of the land and nourished by the sun and rain. These things they believe are given by *Mvelinqangi* whose name literally means 'the-one-who-emerged-first'. He is the Creator of all things and the source of all blessings such as sunshine and rain and children. Usually this Supreme Being is respectfully referred to as *Nkulunkulu* which means the Greatest-of-the-Great. They believe implicitly in his existence and also that their ancestral spirits have the power to intercede on their behalf with *Nkulunkulu*.

The Patriarch

The Zulu live under a patriarchal system. That is, the head of the family is supreme in his authority at home and firmly governs the members of his kraal. Such a household often includes the families of his married sons and perhaps even those of some other dependent relatives in addition to his own wives and children.

The womenfolk, however, have their say in the home itself. Domestic affairs like the organising of food and the care of small children are women's things 'and too trivial for men to be bothered with'. The older children, especially the sons, are disciplined by their fathers who are not usually too strict about trivial matters and natural wildness but are severe in their punishment of irregular behaviour like stealing. In his kraal the father's word is law.

Once in a while, however, a strong-willed wife does emerge and she sometimes challenges him and gets her own way, but this is rather the exception than the rule – such a wife may just as easily end up with a beating for her trouble!

When a crime is committed or a really contentious matter arises in the kraal such as a dispute with a neighbour over grazing rights, this is invariably taken to the local clan chief for judgment. Sometimes in addition the chief is also consulted in domestic matters, like an irreconcilable dispute between a man and his wife. In such an instance, although the chief's word is taken very seriously it need not be final, particularly in the case of young couples because their marriage problems are usually thrashed out with the man's father-in-law.

The Chief

In basic matters of justice or judgment, the Chief's word is accepted as law and according to the doctrine that 'the Chief can do no wrong' his dictates, therefore, remain unchallenged in his own specified territory. He is greatly revered as one who has attained his position by virtue of his heritage. His ancestral spirits, furthermore, are capable of influencing the well-being of the chief's whole clan on earth.

The kind of dispute which he has to settle could for instance arise from a lazy herdboy letting his father's cattle stray into a neighbour's maize patch. In his judgment, the Chief might rule that the owner of the cattle pays the plaintiff a bag of grain. At another time the man's dogs could kill someone else's ewe-in-lamb. The penalty then could perhaps be *five* sheep. This is because the unborn lamb might have been a female lamb which with its mother perhaps would have had that number of lambs in their lifetime.

Hereditary Leadership

In the ascension to the chieftaincy of a clan there may be competition between the heirs of the same lineage, but it would be most unusual for an outsider to contest the seat. The system of voting, as the Western world knows it, is generally unknown in the social system of the country kraals. I heard one old Zulu sum up the idea of it almost indignantly. In his view, it would be disrespectful to suggest that they – the ordinary people – should team up and vote, possibly to replace the son of ancestral forefathers who had always led the clan and who still, as spirits, hold power over their clan and prosper them but could just as easily cause them grief for their disrespect. 'Who are we' he said 'to tell our *Chief* what to do! We must follow *him*, there *is* no other.' That was his expression born from a pattern of life prescribed in the pages of time, long, long before modern civilisation touched him.

This system of patriarchal leadership has the advantages of maintaining discipline and orderliness through all levels of the society, even if at times it is only relative to the strength of the leader himself. Firm and just leadership evokes a sense of loyalty in the tribesman because, basically, the individual Zulu prefers to be led rather than to lead. The inherent disadvantage of this system however, lies in the fact that it stifles initiative and incentive. It inhibits his ability to think for himself so, alone in a crisis, he tends to flounder.

I have outlined the traditional roles of the family head and of the local chief. They are the governors and co-ordinators of daily kraal life. They continue to play a significant role in domestic life although at higher levels today a more sophisticated modern system of administration is evolving.

The King	The king is still the father figure and hereditary sovereign of the nation. His people call him *Ngonyama* or Lion and sometimes he is called *Ndlovu* (elephant). The latter title, however, today appears to be less used except when referring to the past 'father' kings. The idea in using these titles, of course, is to symbolise the great strength and power of the king and arising out of this he is a fountain of great pride to the nation; he is a unifying link which enables the members of nearly three hundred clans to identify themselves as Zulu and to pay ultimate homage to one single sovereign father.

This allegiance to the king of course, started with Shaka, the conqueror, who fired his warriors and the nation he founded with pride and loyalty. The bond between king and subjects has been cemented during the intervening years by the continuing lineage to the present ruler.

Another reason for the king's importance is the unshakeable belief in the power wielded by the royal ancestral spirits over the nation as a whole. These royal spirits can punish at will any of the clans in the entire Zulu nation who displease them or they can reward those who please them. Only the spirits of *royalty* have this power while those of commoners have influence only over their immediate own *families* on earth. Ancestors of clan chiefs, it will be remembered, hold sway over their own clan but not beyond.

The Man and his Home	The Zulu man cherishes and protects his own home jealously. It is his private kingdom and no matter how hospitable he may be to any traveller passing by or kind to any stranger in need of help, no one takes any liberties in his kraal. Family and visitors alike must abide by the time-honoured rules of etiquette. So it is that in KwaZulu today the home is still the hub around which kraal-life revolves. It is, as I have said, the man's kingdom.

To any outsider travelling through the valley or across the hills, these Zulu homes may appear to be very simple and unpretentious. Yet the more I learn of the Zulu, the more conscious I become of what happens behind the scenes. Physically and ethically their system of life has evolved to meet the needs of specific circumstances. The tribesman's code of behaviour is functional and often refined. Unfortunately only those who have an intimate knowledge of the black man's ways, who have stopped to ponder on them and to find reason therein, can detect the refinements in what might outwardly seem to be a haphazard and at times crude way of life.

The Beehive	The traditional Zulu house is a beehive-shaped grass hut with its only opening an arched doorway, about seventy-five centimetres (2½ ft.) high and sixty centimetres (2 ft.) wide, with a removable lattice door made of intertwined wattles. The grass huts normally have no windows, but ventilation is provided by air circulating through the door and filtering out through the thatch. Smoke from a concave fireplace in the mud and cowdung-plastered floor similarly finds its way out. In the process it leaves a deposit of black smoky soot on the thatch which the occupants approve of, because it keeps insects and vermin out of the grass.

Even in the most prosperous families, whose status can be gauged by the number of cattle or other livestock owned by their head, the living quarters consist of separate one-roomed huts. These are not linked or joined in any way to form a multi-roomed building, and as the establishment grows so the accommodation is increased by adding 'beehives' in an orthodox layout common to all traditional Zulu kraals to the extent, naturally, that the contour of their building site permits.

In some areas of KwaZulu, the right type of thatching grass is not always obtainable in sufficient quantity and so the ever-resourceful home-builders have improvised and have used alternative materials such as mud reinforced with stones or wattles for the walls. Thatch is then used only for the roof. However, in some instances, thatch is not used at all, not because it is unavailable but because it is considered more 'with it' to use corrugated iron bought from the trader.

Zulu Architecture

In the orthodox beehive hut, the floor is made of anthill soil crushed up and beaten down hard by the womenfolk of the kraal helped by their neighbours. For this they use round stones which they can comfortably hold in their hands and, where it is available, they add animal fat to the surface to give the floor a sheen. Thereafter at intervals they smear the finished floor with a mixture of cowdung and water to freshen it up and improve its durability.

The building of a Zulu hut, like so many tribal things, is a community affair. All the neighbours – men and women – gather round to lend a willing hand, and within a minimum period of time they complete the structure and each of them shows as much enthusiasm and goodwill as if it were their own home. The host, if he can afford it, is expected to have a supply of home-brewed sorghum beer on tap on such an occasion to keep spirits high, but if he cannot, the work is still done quite happily without any thought of reward.

Sometimes where the housebuilder has not been able to brew sufficient conventional beer due to lack of time, he resorts to a 'quick brew' which is made overnight. This is often as potent as it is quick and may speed up a bunch of merry workers considerably, or if it is plentiful enough may just as easily slow them down into a state of lethargy. This 'instant' brew is made from the usual basic ingredients of meal made from sprouted sorghum or maize, plus yeast, brown sugar and bran. Then, for good measure, a bottle or two of brandy is sometimes thrown in as well.

If the home-owner subsequently decides to move his hut to a spot fairly close by, his friends again come to his rescue. They first loosen the soil around the wattle stakes which secure the structure in the ground and, using their combined strength, pick the entire hut up quite easily and 'walk it' to its new site. As they do so they chant and sing in harmony and the whole exercise becomes a stirring, exciting episode to see.

The furnishing in a hut is minimal because the Zulu sit on goat skins on the floor and they sleep on mats of river rushes which they roll up during the day. In these modern times they buy ordinary blankets from trading stores, but occasionally in some of the older homes blankets made from animal skins are still used. They consistently use home-made clay pots for their beer and sometimes clay dishes for their food but apart from this they invariably have other odds and ends in their huts which have taken their fancy at the trader's store. For instance, enamel plates and dishes and sundry other useful articles like galvanised or plastic water buckets are becoming increasingly popular with the tribesmen. Despite this, in some of the older homes, hand-carved wooden buckets, 'pillows' and spoons have survived to the present day.

Hopefully the potter's craft will not die out in KwaZulu for many years to come. It would indeed be a great pity if the skill of the old craftswomen – for they are the potters – is lost to posterity through indifference to its value and beauty.

The Sacred Msamo

The storage space for the family's goods is at the back of the hut, opposite the doorway. In the case of the main living hut of the head of the family, this storage space or *msamo* is doubly important because it is a place frequented or visited by his family's ancestral spirits. The *msamo* area is usually discernible by a slight ridge which cuts across the curve of the hut in the mud floor at the back, like a slender half-moon.

It is, of course, a particularly religious place and when an offering is made to the spirits then small portions of meat of special religious significance are cut from the offering and hung from the thatch against the wall in the *msamo*. These fragments are intended as refreshment for the spirits who satisfy their hunger by 'licking' them and the Zulu say that this is why the meat there dries out. When they are completely dehydrated, the pieces of meat are ground into a powder and used as 'medicine' to cure various family ailments.

The Man and his Lands

The rural Zulu belongs very much to the soil. He lives close to it. He grows maize and sorghum for food and beer and other crops like pumpkins, melons and tobacco. His wealth lies in the number of cattle which he owns and, apart from these, he breeds goats and invariably has a few black pigs grunting around his kraal amidst the hens and chickens. A Zulu kraal is never complete without a dog – which is usually pathetically thin because he 'must learn to look after himself by hunting for his food'. I find it interesting that Zulu dogs are usually exceptionally obedient. Their owners seldom seem to raise their voices to them but I have often seen these animals come running even at a whispered command. One assumes that they have learnt their lessons the hard way because the Zulu beat their dogs for disobedience and they often end up cringing bundles of nerves, dragging their tails between their legs.

Although the Zulu love livestock and are farmers by nature, their methods are not by any means scientific. By and large, they are averse to change and are suspicious of new ideas like dipping their cattle against disease-carrying ticks and they are often too superstitious to use fertiliser.

Their primary aim in farming is 'quantity rather than quality' and a man would far rather own three scraggy cows producing all together twelve litres of milk than one cow giving the same amount. They have some excuse for this in respect of cattle because a marriage settlement *(lobolo)* for a wife is always calculated in head of cattle so that the numbers are of greater importance than the quality.

In his sowing, the old tribesmen can never resist cramming as many seeds as possible into his land and never seems to appreciate that thinning out would improve his yield. But then, if he should reap more from one bag of seed than his neighbour did from ten over the same area he also stands to lose because he might very easily be accused of using witchcraft. And this can cause serious trouble.

In other ways, too, the better yields resulting from the application of a modicum of science sometimes gives rise to fear and superstition in the countryman's mind. To him it could suggest the work of witches or magic and this makes him wary of using strange methods which he does not really understand, but which some well-meaning person with more education tries to teach him.

Superstitions and a profound belief in the power of witches colours practically every facet of the tribesman's daily life and the effect of this on his farming habits is a case in point. For instance, if the success of a progressive neighbour is attributed to the fact that he is working with witches then he stands to be severely ostracised by his friends and associates.

In an instance which I know of, all farming in a certain valley ceased for months and the crops were literally allowed to die in the field through neglect while a protracted period of mourning was observed after the successive deaths of two or three senior men in the community.

In cases like the death of senior men, the Zulu have many strict taboos in their social code. One of these forbids the tilling of the soil during a period of mourning until offerings have been made to the ancestral spirits in a special cleansing rite. Not until this has happened may they start working in the lands again without the risk of the countryside being completely devastated by hail.

So the benefits of modern scientific farming methods are slow in coming to some of the rural areas. Even those farmers who are themselves progressively inclined and have successfully adopted more modern methods, are hampered by other restrictive factors such as, for example, the tribal rules of protocol which do not permit a tribesman to outshine his chief in any way. In fact, in past times, if a man managed to acquire more cattle than his chief, or have a bigger kraal to house his family, the chief would call in his personal diviner (witchdoctor) to decide whether the man in question was working with witchcraft and magic medicines in his ventures. The outcome was usually an unhappy one for the suspect. Even today, any man would hesitate to build a bigger or better kraal than his chief because, apart from the suggestion that his success was due to witchcraft, it would also indicate that he was boasting superiority over his chief and casting a reflection on his competence.

Arising out of this, it will be seen that the calibre of the chief can have an emphatic influence on life in his clan. An hereditary chief, for instance, may not be a good or progressive leader and as a result can inhibit development in his clan. As an example a young man may go away to study modern agricultural procedures and be ambitious to apply his knowledge on his return home but might instead have to 'play it down' and curtail his enthusiasm so as not to surpass and so offend his chief – and his new-found knowledge may end up by being of no benefit to anyone.

Grain Pits

The tribespeople have always been masters at improvisation – or perhaps it would be more realistic to say that they have invented many surprisingly simple ways to meet essential needs. Their grain pit is an example. Today's sophisticated farmer would hardly think of burying his grain in the ground to preserve it and if, for some reason or another, he did decide to do so he would probably devise the most complicated means of executing the idea. Not so the Zulu farmer who uses a pit in the ground to store his grain. In some Zulu kraals grain pits are still used today but both the art of making them successfully and the need to use them are diminishing because of a growing reliance on the traders to supply their needs in maize. The shiny corrugated iron storage tanks which the traders sell are particularly functional and appeal to the Zulu even if they do not add to the character of their kraals.

The pit is generally used for the long-term storage of the bulk of the annual maize crop which is not needed for immediate use. Pits vary in size according to a family's need and sometimes resemble a small circular underground room with a narrow bottle-neck entrance from above. It seems that some of the best pits of a few years ago were plastered with pottery clay and then fired to give a splendid inside finish with maximum moisture resistance. However, where pits are used today it is more common to plaster the walls thickly with cow-dung. The entrance to the pit is covered at ground level with a good sized flat stone and is well sealed with a plaster of cow-dung.

Traditionally, grain pits are situated inside the cattle byre near the entrance and are under a thick deposit of manure which, when stirred up by the cattle in wet weather, dries out quickly because of its porous nature. In times of danger pits were put outside the byre in inconspicuous places where enemies would not find them easily. The maize required for daily use by the family is kept in little grass huts on stilts inside the family kraal complex behind the hut of a wife. They resemble living huts in design but, of course, are much smaller and, being off the ground, are well ventilated. The inside is accessible through a little doorway at waist-level.

There was quite a surprise awaiting me on the first occasion that I popped my head into one of these apertures. Inside there was a hen, scratching around in the grain. As she rushed out with an awful noise in her panic, she slapped me in the face with her wing and scratched me across my cheek with her toenail.

The Zulu are very tolerant and not at all perturbed by occurences such as fowls nesting in their cool little grain huts and having a free meal or two in the process. The fowls often show their appreciation of this hospitality by leaving an egg in the grain. In seasons of normal rainfall, maize in a good pit should last for at least two years and, according to my informants, even longer than that.

Grain in contact with the walls sometimes goes musty and even mouldy but, at the right stage, this makes very good beer. Deadly poisonous gases do also build up in the pit from time to time but the Zulu are conscious of this and take precautions by leaving a pit open for several hours before attempting to investigate inside. Before doing so they take the added precaution of letting down a fowl, with a cord tied to its legs, into the grain to gauge whether the pit is safe. In researching this subject in KwaZulu, I learnt of a tragic episode where a family carelessly allowed their small son into the grain pit without testing it thinking its gases had dispersed, but he was brought out later, dead. Grain pits have other uses too, and these are not always domestic.

Shaka's Grave

Shaka, the great Zulu king, literally *stands* buried in a grain pit. It is beside a main street in the little town of Stanger which was the site of Shaka's last kraal known as Dukuza. He started the building of Dukuza in 1826 to be nearer his friends, the early white settlers of Port Natal. Numbered amongst these were Nathanial Isaccs, Henry Francis Fynn and Lieutenants Farewell and King.

Shaka loved listening to tales of British exploits and power told to him by these white settlers. In his own mind he built up grand and romantic images of King George IV of England and likened himself to him. Having by now conquered in every direction, Shaka had a burning desire to uplift and educate his nation and make them thinkers in their own right, like the people of 'Mjoji' (his interpretation of George).

Shaka Dies in his Kraal

In previous chapters I have dwelt on the birth and growth of the Zulu nation, on how it was born on the battlefield and nurtured on military conquests and carried to fame on the backs of its mighty warriors. But I want to stress that despite this militaristic background it is nevertheless the kraal and the home which it embodies, which is the ultimate core of the Zulu nation. So it is perhaps more fitting that the founder of this nation should have died and be buried at home in one of his kraals rather than on the battlefield.

Preamble to Death

In more senses than one Shaka hastened his own life to an end at the age of forty-one. He had an iron discipline which enabled him to take life without any hesitation or even a second thought. Yet at other moments he had a deep understanding and compassion for those who needed him. Though he never married, he had an overwhelming affection or love for a few people – men and women. Among these was Ngomane, his Prime Minister and friend from his early years of exile among the Mtetwa. Then there was his favourite warrior and dearest friend Mgobozi of the Hill*. And never to be forgotten was Mpampata, a girl with great intelligence who stood by Shaka through all his years as king, but whom Shaka never married because of a fear that any son he had might challenge his throne. She was like a loving sister to him. Most cherished of all, was Nandi, his mother. She was the greatest influence in his life – so much so, in fact, that her death contributed to his.

When Nandi died, Shaka was demented. He seemed to loose all sense of reason and in a completely irrational and unbalanced attempt to compensate for his loss and atone for his mother's death, he indulged in an unprecedented orgy of killings amongst his own people. Anyone who was not in his view grieving sufficiently was killed; families were massacred *en masse* in their kraals and it is said that during the year of mourning he sent perhaps seven thousand people to 'join the spirit of Nandi'.

Although the Zulu believe firmly that 'the chief can do no wrong' Shaka had now gone too far and had touched the family core too closely. Resentment started to build up among the people and during that ghastly year much of their previous adulation for their leader turned to hatred. Towards the end of the year Shaka mellowed and his friend and adviser, the white elephant hunter and trader Henry Francis Fynn, exerted some influence to persuade him to cease the wanton massacres. But for Shaka it was unfortunately too late. The wheels of intrigue had been set in motion.

Intrigue at Court

As is so often the case in history, the plot against Shaka began at home. His two half-brothers Dingane and Mhlangana, and Mbopa, his erstwhile guard and household chief, conspired to overthrow the king. They were aided and abetted in their plans by Mkabayi, sister of Shaka's father who was determined to place Dingane on the throne. Together they plotted and schemed until at last the opportune moment came when Shaka was exposed. In the belief that no-one would ever challenge his supremacy, he unwisely dispensed with his personal body-guard and in September 1826 he also sent his army off to the North to deal once more with his old enemy, Soshangane of the Ndwandwe. With the army away, Dingane and his accomplices Mhlangana and Mbopa calculated that they would best be able to control the situation and deal with any repercussions which might follow in the wake of an assassination. They set the stage for their foul deed on the eve of the 22nd September 1828.

*Mgobozi earned this title in an illustrious episode on the battlefield.

By a series of clever manoeuvres they managed to get rid of Shaka's attendants and the king was left alone in his cattle byre at a small kraal named KwaNyakamubi adjoining Dukuza. There three deadly assegais were plunged into his body in a matter of moments. Courageous to the last and with unbelievable strength, the dying king was perhaps sad rather than afraid. He rallied his might and in his dying breath remonstrated with the assassins that they should have done this to their own brother. He sagged to the ground and lay still – a mighty ruler fallen.

The throne stood empty. Neither brother had agreed that the other could have it. Mbopa, the erstwhile household guard, stood on the sideline. In their panic the population of Dukuza kraal fled when they heard the news of Shaka's death but in the night dear Mpampata came back undetected and alone to watch over Shaka's body. Through this last act of faith and love she kept at bay the hyaenas which would otherwise have attacked the body during the night.

In the morning when the three assassins returned to the scene, they were astounded to find Shaka's body untouched by the scavenging hyaenas. This completely convinced them that the king had been a supernatural being and they were terrified of the risk of retribution for what they had done, but nevertheless they realised too that Shaka had to be buried and with some semblance of dignity because he was of royal blood. By this time rigor mortis had set in. In addition to the difficulties which this caused there was the problem of disposing of the body quickly and without the aid of grave-diggers. Dingane insisted on according his brother some royal rites and as a concession one black ox was slaughtered to provide the skin in which Shaka's body was wrapped. Thereafter he was placed, standing upright, together with his personal possessions in a conveniently located grainpit in the kraal, thus satisfying both honour and the need for expediency.

Somehow it almost seems appropriate that the great ruler whose energy never waned and whose courage never flagged should make the aquaintance of his spiritual ancestors standing erect on his own feet. The consciences of his assassins might have been less troubled about the unceremonious burial they gave Shaka had they foreseen that a dignified marble statue would one day be erected by a new generation aware of his greatness. The statue, in a mainstreet of Stanger, marks the site of the grain-pit grave of the founder of the Zulu nation and it proclaims to all who pass that way that here stands a man who was indeed a giant among men.

To complete the saga of the Shakan dynasty: Dingane, Mhlangana and Mbopa were well aware of the fact that Shaka's strongest supporters would have to be eliminated quickly. Their first move was against his favourite half-brother, Ngwadi, the young man who had helped Shaka to the throne twelve years before by murdering Sigujana as he bathed in the river. Taken by surprise, Ngwadi fought like a demon and died like a true Zulu warrior in his own kraal, with a pile of dead enemy at his feet. Mpampata, who had come to warn him, surveyed the scene and stabbed herself to death with the little red-handled spear which Shaka had always carried as a hidden means of self-defence.

Jealousy grew between the two brothers – for neither yet had the courage to usurp the throne while the other was alive – and many suspected accomplices on both sides met their deaths. Dingane convinced himself that his own life was in imminent danger and so he schemed and quickly removed all those whom he regarded as possible threats, including Mbopa and his own brother Mhlangana.

Unwisely he let his young brother Mpande live. This was an identical mistake to that which Shaka himself made when he ascended to the Zulu throne; he at that time allowed Dingane to live.

In 1828 Dingane took the Zulu throne. His reign was characterised by intense cruelty which seems to have emanated from a deep-seated desire to emulate his brother, but it developed into a reign of senseless bloodletting within the nation and not much in the way of military conquest. The new Zulu king lacked Shaka's wisdom, his finesse and his statesmanship. He ruled his people by fear and with little justice.

The Years of Twilight

With Shaka's death the sun went down on an era of great achievement and the glory with which he had gilded the Zulu name lost much of its lustre. Whilst the power of the nation did not diminish, its reputation certainly suffered. The pride which Shaka had instilled into his warriors was now largely replaced by fear of their new leader.

The twilight lasted in Dingane's Zululand for twelve years until the so-called 'simpleton' Mpande, the young brother whom Dingane had not rated as a danger, ousted him with the aid of the Boers and seized the throne in 1840. Dingane fled to the far North where he was subsequently murdered by local tribesmen.

Mpande brought peace and quiet to the land for thirty-two uneventful years. This was a period of dusk and of rest before a new dawn and a reawakening of the Zulu which came with the advent of Mpande's son, Cetshwayo in 1873.

Cetshwayo put excitement back into the veins of his warriors and revived their pride in being Zulu. He gave them the glory of their great victory at Isandlwana and the excitement of the battle at Rorke's Drift which was an epic of gallantry by both Zulu and British alike. But sadly the events proved to be the beginning of the end for Cetshwayo, the last of the warrior kings of Zululand.

Back to the Kraal

What then has happened to the descendants of these illustrious warriors of yesteryear, the memory of whose exploits and adventures still stir the imagination of story-tellers? We will take a closer look at these 'People of the Sky' in their present homeland where ancient traditions and modern innovations are the contenders, side by side, in a new kind of battle.

Chapter 5

Life in the 20th Century Kraal

The way of life in the Zulu kraal appears in essence to any outsider to be simple and uncomplicated with the inhabitants going about their daily affairs and systematically following a routine which appears to be quite uneventful and straightforward.

In reality and behind the scenes, the lives of these unsophisticated and largely illiterate people are affected by many complexities. Their seemingly rough social system encompasses on the one hand a set of fine ethical codes which would be a credit to any society and on the other, a number of practical habits founded on sound common sense harnessed to meet the needs of everyday living. Routine daily patterns of life and entrenched behavioural codes tend to create an impression that life in the kraals is uncomplicated, but behind this facade a multitude of intricate superstitions and beliefs lies hidden. In many respects they make the tribesman's life anything but simple.

Taboos What complicates his life is the fact that there are two distinct sides to it. Firstly the purely physical, and secondly the spiritual combined with the magical. These two facets are, in fact, so inextricably linked that many physical activities within a Zulu community are ultimately governed by the dictates of various supernatural forces and rigid taboos.

These taboos affect the management of everyday affairs in a kraal in many ways and they influence many aspects of life from birth to death. As an example: if a man earmarks an ox for sacrifice to his ancestral spirits, then he no longer regards it as his own, but *their* property. 'They' guard it jealously and if he should weaken and dispose of it for mere money or other reasons he would court disaster, perhaps even death, for depriving them of their sacrifice and meat. Taboos are rigorously applied to the eating of sour milk and other foods under specific conditions.

Apart from continuously wanting to be remembered by their living families – as ancestral spirits do – they periodically 'get hungry for meat' and make their demands known through dreams by members of their living family. When I asked about the eating habits of the spirits, I was told that they *need* 'sustenance' just like we do and 'they eat the things we eat', not only meat and beer but other food too. The Zulu put little fragments of any food down for them on special occasions in places like the cattle byre, and the spirits 'lick' it – 'but they take so little you can hardly notice that they have eaten.' Sometimes the people even drop small pieces of meat in the fire for them.

At a beer drink it is common to see a man pour a little of his beer on to the ground in the cattle byre before he has his own first sip. This is for the spirits when they frequent the byre which is a sacred place. The affection which the spirits have for the byre seems to be a perpetuation into the next world of the great love the living man himself has for it as the place of his beloved cattle. Another example of the taboos practised in the kraals is that which decrees that a man who has had sex the night before is contaminated, and may not embark on certain projects the next day or even participate in certain tribal rites because he is unclean and likely to jeopardise the success of the project concerned.

The Superior Sex

Zulu men regard themselves as the superior sex. The head of the home, in particular, is paid respect in numerous ways. In his advancing years he ranks as a spirit in his actual lifetime and may have sacrifices of cattle offered to him. Apart from that, he is continuously honoured, not only by his wife, but by his daughters and daughters-in-law and by any other women in the kraal.

In the Zulu language this act of paying respect is called *hlonipha*. It takes so many forms that some of the acts have simply become part of everyday family etiquette. One conspicuous form of *hlonipha* is that practised by brides. After they marry they wear a headdress which sometimes comes down so far over their forehead that they have to tilt their heads back to be able to see ahead. I have heard it said of a bride's veil that it is so 'that she may not look her father-in-law in the eye until she has presented him with a grandchild and proved her worth as a wife and as a woman'. The husband for his part also gets an adequate share of respect from her. The particular form a bride's headdress takes depends on the fashion of the tribe concerned and may be a cloth or some form of beaded fringe.

As a non-Zulu and a white man, I have often experienced incidents where respect in one form or another has been paid to me by the tribespeople. At my home in Pretoria for instance, we have a housemaid who is a second generation urban Zulu in that her father before her came to live and work in a Transvaal town. Apart from being removed from Zulu country, she is actually urban-bred. Much Zulu culture, however, still runs in her blood and no doubt will even be passed on to her city son for perpetuation by him. For instance, she frequently delivers some or other message to me or announces a visitor without crossing the threshold of my study. When I first became conscious of her habit I wondered what the reason for it was, but I felt I would be lacking in finesse if I questioned her. One day, however, the answer emerged quite spontaneously when she told me about the bad manners of some little Zulu boy who had had his ears boxed by his father for running into his private hut without first asking permission to enter. 'You see', she said, 'the things in that room are the father's things only so if anyone else wants to go in there he must be up to mischief, otherwise why would he go in?' She summed it up with 'the privacy of the head of a family must be *respected*'.

A Visitor for the Family Head

A custom which never ceases to intrigue me is the procedure by which a strange visitor is received at a kraal. It originated in earlier, much tougher days, when enemies of different clans had the habit of stealthily murdering their victims at moments when they were at their most vulnerable. The procedure for the reception of a stranger almost certainly started as a device for protection but has now developed, I think, into a means of drawing attention to the dignity and importance of the head of the family and to the necessity of showing him respect. Etiquette is important in the kraal and a visitor, particularly a male, must be announced to the head of the home with proper formality. This involves a procedure which is inconspicuous to anyone not knowing Zulu custom and is very subtly executed. The basic idea is to protect the family head and to avoid his being taken by surprise by a visitor bent on mischief.

When a stranger arrives at a kraal he is unlikely to see the head of the kraal in any conspicuous place, and if he does, he should never barge in and approach him directly. Etiquette demands that he enter the kraal through its main gateway, that is the *sango* in the stockade which usually surrounds the huts of a kraal. There he must turn right and move up the passageway between the outer stockade and that of the cattle byre – which is a smaller enclosure within the main one. There he must address himself to some lesser person like a wife or a child and ask them if the head of the home is in. The family member concerned immediately proceeds to 'protect' her master from the stranger – who might be an enemy – with evasive tactics. They say, for instance, 'Well he was here early this morning, but then he went to the lands. I'll find out if anyone knows where he is.' With ultra caution, the family member then goes by a devious way to the father in his hut, or wherever he may be, and describes the visitor to him.

If he is satisfied with the caller's credentials, the father sends a message back to the effect that he is busy at the moment but is coming. He then keeps his visitor waiting for a while even if he is doing nothing, because it would suggest his inferiority if he hurried. After he has delayed long enough to impress the newcomer, he eventually appears but his attitude at the outset is very formal if the visitor is a stranger. He asks questions about the other's health and his place of residence and his crops and, ultimately, the pertinent question: 'Why are you so far away from home and what brings you to these parts?' These preliminaries normally relax both parties and they'll eventually settle down to a friendly chat which might last for hours because time is meaningless to the average man of the kraals. Eventually when such a visitor leaves, he must take his exit by the left side passageway leading back to the front gate of the kraal, that is along the opposite side from that by which he came in.

An interesting piece of information linked with the subject of a man's enemy is that the old Zulu say that the purpose in building their hut doors so low is to prevent an enemy from easily coming in while the household is asleep and killing someone. With the low door the intruder runs a risk in that he has to bend so low to enter it that he is not only momentarily helpless, but he also leaves his back exposed for the head of the home to stab.

Family Duties

The Zulu man is polygamous and has the privilege by Zulu law of taking as many wives as he can afford to raise *lobolo* cattle for. He may also have unmarried sweethearts in addition to his wives if he wishes. This liberty or pleasure is denied to his wives who dare not have even a mild affair with another man except at a heavy risk of dire consequences or even death if they are discovered.

In the Zulu kraal the family's womenfolk ordinarily do the major share of the housework but the men do their share of the heavier tasks where physical strength is necessary. Fathers and their sons take a pride in tending the family's cattle and other livestock, but as this does not take all day they are not averse to sitting idly in the sun when duties are not so pressing – and pressing tasks are not over-common in the hills far away from the hurly-burly of so-called 'civilisation'. I once met a man with five or six wives and even more daughters-in-law in his kraal and he told me that he had not been out of his valley for years, not even to the nearby trader's store. 'When I was young,' he said, 'yes. But why should I work now when I have so many women to look after my affairs.'

He made it quite clear that it would be undignified for him to toil now and it would be an adverse reflection on his prestige and a denial of his prosperity. Nevertheless in the spring after it has rained it is usually the man of the kraal who ploughs the lands, helped by his sons. He also plants his crop which is most likely to be maize or sorghum or both, with a few melons or pumpkins thrown in.

In some regions the Zulu also grow beans and potato-like tubers they call *madumbe*, which are of the genus *arum*. Once crops are planted the wives and daughters have to hoe the lands and keep them free of weeds or perhaps it would be best to say 'relatively free', because tribal farmers are not normally as conscientious about their farming as it would pay them to be. While his wives and daughters hoe, it is customary for the old patriarch to stroll over to his lands and scold them intermittently for the way in which they work. Sometimes his criticism is justified, but often it is just to remind them of his authority and importance and of their duty to obey and respect him. Despite these prerogatives the Zulu man has tremendous vitality and strength when the need arises for him to use it.

Among their other duties, the women of the kraal carry water for the home from the nearest river or other source and they gather wood for the home fires too. As in the case of most or all of Southern Africa's tribeswomen, they are able to carry incredibly heavy loads balanced on their heads apparently as effortlessly as if they were no heavier than a bottle of paraffin. They walk along laughing and joking with their companions for many kilometres from kraal to trading store and back. One obvious result of carrying goods on their heads in this way is the splendid deportment which most tribal women develop and which gives them an almost regal bearing. Duties are allocated to the female members of the family from an early age and one of the major tasks of the young girls in the kraal is to act as nursemaid. Not only do they attend to the children of their own homes, but also to those of their neighbours if help is needed. This is in accordance with the unwritten Zulu code of unselfishly helping one another when and wherever help is needed.

Boys for their part are father's aides – they milk the cows and herd the livestock in their proper grazing areas to keep them away from the neighbour's crops because lands are seldom fenced.

The Divided Hut

The layout of a Zulu kraal follows a basic pattern which will be discussed elsewhere, but it is appropriate to mention here that even in the single hut which is the home of a married couple, etiquette plays a part. It decrees a division of the interior into 'his' and 'hers'! Looking in from the doorway towards the *msamo* (or storage area) at the back of the hut, the right side is the husband's area and the left his wife's.

Many aspects of life in the kraal, particularly those involving priorities and rights, are governed by this division between the right hand and the left hand and the man invariably explains this point by flexing his right arm muscles and clenching that fist to emphasise a reference to the side which carries the strength. Later it will be related how in polygamous marriages this yardstick is a major factor.

In this system of the division of the hut, the man occupies his own side and she hers and when they have visitors the males and females separate accordingly. Even in sleeping they keep to their own sides unless on occasion *he* feels that she is in the wrong place!

This may all seem somewhat rigid but I never fail to think of the affection evidenced between an aged married couple I encountered. Their pillows told the story. In their hut there were two separate wooden 'pillows' joined by a 2-metre long continuous chain of wooden links so that the whole outfit was indivisible. It was all carved out of a single tree-trunk and allowed the man to sleep on his side of the hut and his wife on hers. They remained symbolically united even in sleep.

Diet

In small new homes, the cooking is often done inside the living hut in the open fireplace on the floor, or in good weather, outside in the open. Established homes have a separate hut in the kraal complex which is used as a kitchen. Most of the food for a family is boiled in a three-legged cast-iron pot, but items like meat and maize on the cob when it is in season, are often roasted on the coals. When meat is roasted as a variation it is frequently scorched almost black on the outside and left very rare inside. Unlike white people, who like their corn on the cob tender and succulent, the Zulu eat theirs hard and at the stage where chewing it is hard work.

Maize is their most popular diet and they eat it in various forms. One popular way is to grind it to a meal in a concave stone using another round stone held in their hands to mill it. Then they cook it into a stiff, lumpy porridge which they eat from chunks held in their hands. The process of grinding maize has been made a lot easier in latter years for the tribespeople because many of the country stores have installed motorised mills where the customers' needs can be met by grinding, free of charge, the maize which they grow in their own fields. They can also buy ready-ground maize-meal from traders and other stores. As an alternative to roasting maize on the cob, the tribespeople often shell the grain after it is completely dry and then boil it for at least a day and eat it as whole grain. When they have curdled milk available they use this with it. This form of eating maize provides splendid exercise for the jaw muscles!

Zulu people are particularly partial to sour milk. They call it *amasi* and say it makes 'a man strong and desired'! They never drink milk fresh although as recently as a few years ago little boys were adept at milking cows directly into their mouths. But the older men say today that 'boys are not now what they used to be. They have completely lost this art and with it the fun that it involves.'

The only other time the people of the kraals use fresh milk or 'green milk' as they call it, is to thin down curdled milk which has become too thick to eat by itself.

Most of the taboos of the kraals are tied to rules which necessitate an abstention from the taking of sour milk or *amasi*. As an example, common occurences like menstruation or someone's contact with death, are regarded as sources of contamination and the person connected or concerned has to be purified by various procedures, including abstention from *amasi*. Such taboos are eventually lifted by a lapse of time and usually also by cleansing ceremonies in which the person affected is purified by specified rituals.

To return to the subject of diet as such, a dish which is popular in many parts of KwaZulu is dry beans boiled together with maize. In different areas, however, the people have preferences for specific varieties of beans and one trader in the Eshowe area told me that he has customers who walk long distances to his store to purchase one particular type of bean whenever he has it in stock. They cannot pronounce the English name for it and have given it one of their own.

The Zulu have few inhibitions and discuss any subject with complete frankness. Their language is noted for its idiomatic descriptions and they call these particular beans 'thundering buttocks'!

Mealtimes are twice a day: when the sun is at about ten or eleven o'clock (the rural tribespeople are mostly illiterate and cannot tell the time), and in the evening. Enamel plates have become popular in many homes but older families still have little pottery bowls for wet food and elongated hand-carved, wooden plates for meat. For serving, they traditionally have large wooden hand-made ladles like oversized spoons. Then they have a much smaller spoon which they use mostly for eating curdled milk. Both Zulu pottery and wood-carvings have ornamental designs on them. Pottery is done by the women and wood-carving by men.

Cockroaches

In addition to these utensils, small woven grass mats are used in some cases for eating dry foods on the hut floor where the family sit. A problem with these, however, is that fragments of food foul up the crevices and make them difficult to clean and to keep hygenic. In the old days, some tribes liked to have cockroaches around because they cleaned out the deposits in their grass food mats and with this in mind I one day asked a Zulu man what *his* people thought of cockroaches. He shuddered visibly and in a few words told me the Zulu realise that cockroaches do a good job but they do *not* like them! He said that when a cockroach falls into the milk, they give it to the children because 'children don't care, but if it falls in the beer, well, that's too good to waste!'

Beer

Beer (*tshwala*) is almost as inseparable a part of the Zulu way of life as is breathing. This, of course, holds good in the case of all the other rural black people of Southern Africa. Not that they are continuously drinking beer, but it is an essential part of every ceremony or feast. A pot of beer provides a warm, welcoming gesture to any friend or visitor, but perhaps most important of all, it is the food which they give to their ancestral spirits to satisfy *their* thirst and at the same time to prove to them, the ancestral spirits, that they have not been forgotten by their families back on earth. This is a pleasant way of reminding the spirits that they are remembered because after the priest (usually the head of the family) has made the offering by pouring a small quantity on to the ground in the byre, he and his guests drink the rest.

At other times beer is brewed purely for a party, without there being any religious connotation attached to the process. No host would think of entertaining guests in his home without serving beer if he has had time to prepare it, and no social occasion is complete without it. There are many rituals and customs connected with the brewing and the serving of beer which are faithfully kept. This is so important that even in South Africa's cities where there are many state-sponsored breweries which scientifically brew traditional tribal beer to satisfy the taste of the black people, great care is taken to retain the taste, colour and qualities of the kraal product. It is provided for them, the black people, at a nominal cost and as a facility designed especially for their pleasure and benefit.

Origin of the Tribesman's Beer

The early Natal pioneer and friend of Shaka, Henry Francis Fynn, refers in his diary to beer and mentions the *mabele* corn and *phoko* grain which was grown in Shaka's time specially for the purpose of making beer. He described this as 'a most pleasant beverage which sometimes intoxicates the drinker'. But in the

DAILY LIFE

Little boys are the herdsmen of a kraal.

Left: Grain storage 'bags' like these are a rarity very seldom seen among the Zulu of today. The grass covers in the case of all three are a protection against the weather and are removable. The stick protruding in the near left-hand corner from the thatch is treated with magic medicine to keep the lightning away.

Right: Near Tugela Ferry, the South African Government has created a scheme for the local residents to irrigate their lands. The maize partly visible on the left is an illustration of the reward they reap. Zulu women customarily tend the crops.

Left: Ploughing after the spring rains.

Right: Taking maize out of the family's grain storage pit in the cattle byre. The woman's skirt is of cowhide and is of a type popular over a large area. The head-dress worn by the woman with the hoe is a fixture being made up of coarse knitting wool interwoven with her own hair; that of the other is a 'wig' which may be removed at night.

Beer – the delight of any man.

A medicine man treating a patient.

Rawhide thongs or riems are essential for inspanning oxen and many other everyday needs. A dry, unsalted hide is cut into a long circular strip. This is wound over a bough and weighted down with a rock. A length of wood, as seen here, is stuck into the thong and the owner walks round winding the hide up tightly. He then removes the stick, to let the thong spin back to the ground. The process is repeated in the opposite direction and so on until the riems are soft and pliable. They are sometimes rubbed with fat, to soften them.

Leatherwork is a craft
usually practised by
individual specialists among
the people of the kraals.
This man is wearing a soft,
beautifully tanned kaross
made by him, at the same
time as he makes shields of
tough, hard, sun-dried hide.

Beer is always brought on by the women to the men. The married woman on the left – distinguishable by her head-dress and leather skirt – has an empty drinking pot while the girl carries the beer in a collared pot which prevents spillage.

122

The drummers in the background relax while an exhausted dancer is given their affection by the kraal's dogs.

A young man marks out a new shield on an ox-hide.

Getting the 'feel' of their drum.

In spite of the weight and encumbrance of his best party outfit this man could not resist practising his dance movements.

Caught in the process of rubbing his legs down with a piece of stone, this man insisted on showing me precisely how he washes.

This woman is conspicuous because of her beadwork which is unique in both the pattern and colour. The tattoo marks on her face are 'a custom of her family'. If the custom is not kept up, the person is likely to incur the displeasure of the ancestral spirits and grow ill.

early 1600's, long before Shaka, indigenous tribes of Nguni in the far north were familiar with the excellent quality of sorghum grain for consumption either in liquid or in solid forms. Bryant traces the introduction of maize in the diet of the Zulu people to the time when their progenitors moved away and settled further south. Here they found that the variety of grain which they had used in the north did not do very well, especially as a foodstuff. They concentrated on growing sorghum for brewing purposes only, and cultivated maize for eating. They discovered it when they made contact with the Portuguese. Today sorghum is still the basic ingredient used in the malting process of tribal home-brewed beer but sprouted maize and maizemeal is often used with it or as an alternative. In some branches of the Zulu nation, in the northern areas, they also make a brew from the sap of a fan-palm tree which they call the *lala* palm. In their language *lala* means to sleep, so no doubt the tree got its name originally from the soporific delights which its juices gave to those who partook of them.

Beer Recipe

In all Zulu homes, the families brew their own beer or *tshwala* as they call it and the method of making it is an old traditional one which is basically common to most of the tribes of southern Africa. It has, though, been necessary in different areas to adapt brewing methods and malting procedures to suit local climatic conditions and the species of grain which grows best in those parts.

In the process of beer making there are several specific steps; the first is the sprouting of the corn which is done by laying it between wet sacks or rush mats for a few days until the grains become fat and swollen and have sent out healthy new sprouts. When the latter are about a centimetre long and beginning to turn green, the corn is taken from the sacks and laid in the hot open sunlight. The sprouts shrivel and die into brown coir-like appendages and the corn hardens and shrinks back to size.

This dry sprouted corn is called *imithombo*. It is now ground into powdered malt in a concave milling stone by the women of the home using smooth oval river stones somewhat bigger than a tennis ball held in the hand. This in turn is mixed with water into a thin porridge-like substance, technically known as wort or dough. It is the catalyst or fermentation agent. The beer is now made by boiling the wort and adding further dry malt, maize-meal and water to it in various proportions until the mixture is of the desired consistency. Apart from boiling, the mixture also has to stand at intervals to ferment. It ends up as a pinkish brew with a thin-porridge texture and is covered on the surface with a layer of fine husks which are strained out by squeezing the mixture through loosely woven tubular grass strainers about sixty cm. (2 ft.) long which are twisted by the operator to force the liquid through the sieve. The Zulu call these strainers *mahluzo*.

Beer-brewing in its entirety is women's work, but care has to be taken to ensure that the women are not 'contaminated' at the time they make it because if anyone of them has, for instance, indulged in sex on the night before the beer will turn out insipid and flat.

Once the brewing is complete beer has a short life and that made from sorghum malt begins to sour after about forty-eight hours. Maize-beer has an even shorter life and is said to begin deteriorating after its first day. Beer drinks usually end up as exceedingly merry occasions, but this is probably due to the large quantities which the tribespeople consume at a time rather than to the strength of the brew. The alcoholic content of normal beer is very low and is said seldom to exceed 2%, although some modern brewers have found that they can liven it up considerably by adding sugar during fermentation or even a bottle or two of brandy.

Beer for the Ancestral Spirits

The traditional courtesies and customs associated with beer drinks and drinking are varied and too numerous to discuss in any detail here. I do, however, wish to dwell briefly on the subject to illustrate the important part beer plays in kraal life. Firstly, it is the national brew of the Zulu and is made by those who can afford it as a luxury beverage for the benefit of the family and their guests. But then it is also made for ritual ceremonies and used as an offering to ancestral spirits. For major occasions where, for instance, serious illness or death are concerned, goats or an ox are also offered with it to placate the spirits and calm any displeasure they may be exhibiting.

Legends

There are some fascinating legends about old traditional festivals from Zulu history and some of which, I believe, are still practised in more remote Zulu communities even today. The feast of the Chieftainess of the Skies or Goddess of Grain is one. Her name is Nomkhubulwana. She is an exciting being and there are some mysterious and interesting facets attached to the legend about her. She is a somewhat similar character to Ceres, the Roman Corn Goddess. She visits earth in the Spring of each year and expects to find little pots of specially-brewed beer left for her by the girls of the area in the fields which they have tilled during the day. They only give her a minute portion of the total of the beer they brew and the rest is drunk at home by the family with much relish in anticipation of the good crops they expect the goddess to bring them.

Beer is also used as a balm to make peace between two old enemies. The men concerned embark on a special washing or cleansing ceremony. They refer to it as 'pouring water over each other' (*ukuthelelana amanzi*) and then they exchange palm leaves or other tokens of goodwill before they sit down on a mat together and drink beer from a single special pot to show that they are reconciled.

Another old custom is that practised in the winter in the off-work season, when local kraals take turns at having 'open house' beer feasts where all and sundry join in. Here they follow many courtesies and one rule is that no-one except the *pater familias* of the kraal may start drinking until the local headman or chief arrives. As the family head, he is given his own pot of beer or *khamba* in his hut in the early morning and he starts his drinking then. After the headman or chief has arrived, the beer is ladled out from the fermentation pots with long-necked gourd ladles by the girls of the kraal into drinking pots and then taken to the visiting men who share a pot between three or four of them. The girls then serve the women guests who sit in a separate hut, or on a patch of grass on their own. Before serving beer, the girls take the scum and flies off the top with grass strainers, then swallow large mouthfuls of beer themselves to satisfy everyone that all is in order. At smaller parties the family head does this preliminary tasting himself to prove that it is not poisoned or 'doctored' in any evil way.

These points I have mentioned are purely isolated illustrations of the role of beer in kraal life but they do, perhaps, give some indication of its importance in daily Zulu life.

Chapter 6
Growing Up

Almost every facet of their lives reflects the Zulu belief in powers greater than their own. The birth of a child is an example of this.

Nkulunkulu's Gift of a Baby

They say a child is a *special* blessing bestowed on them by *Nkulunkulu,* the Creator. Once having sent his gift, *Nkulunkulu* does not influence the child's daily affairs – the family's ancestral spirits do that – although he might show his hand in subsequent *major* events in the child's life. For instance, *Nkulunkulu* might pluck him out of the hands of death in an accident or he might on another day show him the path when he is lost in a perilous place. The Zulu marvel when such things happen and say: 'Hawu! *Nkulunkulu* kept him safe!'

Choice of Sex

I have often asked Zulu parents whether they prefer to have sons or daughters and they have invariably replied, 'We don't mind which it is.'

Because daughters bring wealth to the family one might have expected them to show a preference for girls, but they are humbly grateful for whatever the Creator gives them and would never be so ungracious as to suggest that He had cheated them. They are also quite philosophical in their reasoning that if the first-born is a girl it does not really matter, because sooner or later there will be a son.

It is, of course, something of a tragedy if a father never has a son because he, the father, needs sons to help him in the male duties of his kraal, to care for him in his old age and above all to be his heir and ultimately take over the leadership of his family when he, himself, 'goes back home'.

But over and above these physical considerations, a father feels an overriding necessity to produce a male descendant in order that his family line may be perpetuated in the ranks of his ancestral spirits and its continuity ensured.

Daughters, for their part, are rejoiced in for the help they give their mothers and fathers and because they are 'father's wealth' as 'the cattle of the family'. This is a reference to the father's potential gain when one day his daughter will be taken in marriage against a 'bride price' or *lobolo* in cattle which the bridegroom will bring him.

Twins

The Zulu attitude towards twins is beautifully summarised in his book 'The Zulu People' by that eminent authority on the Zulu and other cultures, Dr A. T. Bryant. He writes: 'This twin business seems to have been a phenomonen that rather puzzled and frightened humanity right up from its earliest days. Right around the world . . . twins were universally regarded as something decidedly suspect to say the least, yet exceptionally they were welcomed with joy.'

The Zulu are no exception in their concept of twins. They used to kill one and sometimes even both of the children even though they considered them as having been specially sent by the ancestral spirits. The reason for this action which appears to be in direct conflict with the designs of their family's spirits, seems to have been their deep-rooted fear of the unnatural and they place twins in this category. In the same way it was Zulu custom to dispose of abnormal or deformed babies. In the 19th century, however, it seems these customs began to die out of the people's own accord and then, in addition, the advent of the white man's law accelerated the change until the old procedures became largely or perhaps entirely extinct.

There is evidence that some of the less enlightened tribespeople in various regions of Africa still today retain traces of uneasiness and fears of the supernatural when twins are born. I believe that they treat them with special medicines to immunise them against certain dangers and also, because they are 'unnatural beings', steps have to be taken to prevent them from affecting other people. Outwardly Zulu twins apparently grow up and run around today much in the same way as ordinary children do and they are basically treated in the same way, but older and more superstitious parents still lack the courage to administer corporal punishment to twins when they have been recalcitrant for fear of some form of retribution from the spirits.

When I asked members of the *Ntombela* clan near Nqutu and of the Mpungose near Eshowe about their attitude to twins, the reply in both cases was: 'We like them. They are a double blessing from the ancestral spirits. We kill an ox or a goat for our ancestral spirits as soon as the children are born. That is to say "thank you" to them.'

This sacrifice of an animal was made even in the old days before the then 'twin custom' changed and the meaning of the offering is probably a lot deeper than is now understood. It possibly embodies a supplication for protection from supernatural forces, because in the old days it was believed that danger, like the death of the father, was inherent in the advent of twins.

The suggestion above that twins are a special blessing from the *ancestral spirits* does not necessarily mean that they are in any way less of a gift from *Nkulunkulu*. The ancestral spirits have communication with the Creator, and therefore have probably acted as intermediaries.

Irrespective of any general statements of the pleasure that the birth of twins brings, I personally feel that old beliefs and customs and superstitions die hard among the tribespeople and that a twin walks in an aura of a type all its own. For instance, the Zulu say that 'a person suffering from a stiff neck, must have it twisted by a twin and none other and it will immediately be cured'.* When they add the number of souls in their family, the Zulu do *not* include twins because this would bring them bad luck.

Family Size

The rural Zulu have large families and rejoice in fertility. They are not orientated towards birth control between man and wife. Families of eight and ten children are common and, in polygamous marriages, they are usually many more. Irrespective of family size, however, Zulu parents bring their children up strictly and discipline them admirably in manners, etiquette and codes of honour. But they do not stifle them. They let them learn to look after themselves, to be independant and self-reliant from an early age. Mother Nature has many lessons to teach children and Zulu parents allow theirs to roam the paths of her varied and beautiful gardens at will. There they learn things of great value in life.

*Bryant's *Zulu-English Dictionary*.

Baby's First Lessons The people of the kraals like their babies to walk by the time they are about nine months old. At about this age they start lifting them on to their feet to teach them to stand. If a child proves to be lazy and does not start to walk when it is expected to, some of the more custom-minded parents try other methods. I have been told that one old custom was to make small incisions in a child's knees so that it hurt him to crawl and he was forced to try and get up. Another old custom was to sit the child on an anthill of a certain type of ant which bites when disturbed. This 'makes the child get up'! I have, however, not discovered any cases of this still happening among the people of today but I would be hesitant to say that in some remote corners it does not. This would probably be the exception rather than the rule. One old custom still prevalent today and likely to remain so is the one whereby a mother weans her child by rubbing the bitter sap of an aloe on her nipples. The Zulu say that this never fails to work.

Choosing a Name The tribespeople, unlike their white counterparts, do not have a collection of common first names to draw on for their children; names are selected at random. Parents often display great originality in their choice and a common practice is for them to invent a name which links the child to some important happening or occasion at the time of its birth.

For instance, I know of one case where a baby girl was born a few days after her father had been involved in a severe accident which temporarily immobilised him. When his family brought him the news in his hut of the birth of the baby, he asked, 'Is it a boy or a girl?' They replied: 'It is a girl,' and he said, 'Her name will be *Nozingozi*.' This means in effect 'Miss Accident'. The prefix 'No' is a title of courtesy for a female irrespective of whether she is married or not. It is equivalent to the English/American designation Ms. Had the 'accident child' been a boy, his equivalent name would simply have been *Zingozi* (Accident). Such names are the person's first name or the equivalent of a Christian name. A person's clan or sib name is his surname. In this case this was *Simango,* which is an off-shoot of the *Nkomonde* so her name is Nozingozi kaSimango kaNkomonde. The word *Simango* is borrowed from the Xhosa language and is their name for a species of monkey and *Nkomonde* in Zulu means 'cattle that are long' (enduring). Translated then, the little girl's name is 'Miss-Accident-Monkey-of-long-Cattle'.

Another way in which the tribespeople choose names for their children is to keep their ears open for a word, say, from English which has a pleasant sound; or it might even be a phrase. One man I know rejoices in the name of 'Deepfreeze' and another in that of 'Nextweek'. But I have come across one name which surpasses all others. I do not think its bearer is a full Zulu, but that is irrelevant. His father, at the time of his birth, apparently worked in a city for an electrical contracting firm and had obviously had some schooling, otherwise he would never have been able to cope with the name which he chose for his son. It is: 'Overheadlinedirectioncontrolsign'. The young man who owns it says, 'But my mother she not like that name . . . she just call me Beauty.'

The principle of relating a name to a major event often serves a useful purpose in later years in that it helps estimate a man's age where he is illiterate and does not himself know exactly how old he is in years. For example, if he was born in a year when a major flood took place and had the name of *Mvulankulu* (meaning 'Rain that is Big') then later anyone could pinpoint the year of his birth, but not the exact day if it was a prolonged rain.

The name a boy is given by his family at birth is always used in family circles and by his parents and his contemporaries, but in practice he may earn several new names in his lifetime. At puberty he is given a name by his friends which they use, and if he subsequently becomes a hero at, for instance, stick-fighting his friends will give him a praisename which acclaims this feat.

Added to these naming procedures, there are many other complexities in the Zulu system: For example, at times they use 'son-of-so-and-so' who was the son of 'so-and-so', but these aspects of names are too technical to describe in greater depth here.

'A Child of the Spirits'

Sometimes a family's ancestral spirits lay claim to a child and jealously dictate how certain affairs in his or her life should be handled. This often happens where a particular spirit has reason to be attached to and particularly fond of a child or one of its parents.

One instance of which I know concerns a woman who had an aunt by marriage (not a blood-relation) who idolised her when she was a little girl. This aunt said that when the child grew up, it *had* to marry a Zulu of her (the aunt's) particular clan. The girl grew up and instead of marrying a Zulu, she went away and married a Tswana man of the sib *Mekwe* and became *Mekwe* too.

During the next few years she unfortunately had four miscarriages and no living child of her own. She and her husband were nervous and superstitious and called in a diviner. The diviner went into a deep coma and spoke to the spirits and came back with the answer that the wife's spiritual ancestor-aunt was still upset that her niece had not married a Zulu. But she told the diviner that if her niece would promise to make the child a Zulu by giving it the name of its deceased grandfather, she would conceive and bear a child. In due course the woman gave birth quite naturally to a healthy boy and instead of taking his Tswana father's name of Mekwe, he was given his Zulu grandfather's full name of *Abram Simango*. Today he is a healthy boy of fifteen and is his mother's pride and joy. He is known as a 'Child of the Spirits' and he is their property.

Another case I encountered concerned a grown-up Zulu man who had the name of *Jabula,* meaning 'rejoice'. But, instead of rejoicing, he was continuously ill. He also went to a diviner and was told that an old ancestor who liked him was resentful because he had not been given *his* (the ancestor's) name of *Nyamakazi* – which is more Xhosa than Zulu and means 'wild buck'. Jabula immediately changed his name and ever since has been a fit man except that he has a great fear that someone might mistakenly use his old name and upset his ancestral guardian once more.

Early Years

In the first years of their lives little Zulu children are seldom short of nurse-maids because, apart from their own mother, they have the bigger girls of their homes and of the neighbourhood to carry them around, tied to their backs with a blanket. From the time they are hardly more than toddlers themselves, little girls are taught to 'piggy-back' the babies of the kraals.

Little boys begin to go out from about five years old with their bigger brothers to herd their father's goats and cattle. They take the animals to the grazing field, keep them out of unfenced crop lands during the day and bring them back home in the evening to be milked and penned for the night.

This may appear to be an idyllic, uncomplicated way of growing up – but beneath the surface, it has its hazards like a good beating for neglect of duties.

Up to the age of puberty boys traditionally run around naked in the warm sunshine, but Westernisation is rapidly changing this as well as many other facets of the tribesman's life. Now, frequently, they wear short trousers but usually nothing else. Little girls wear bead aprons from the beginning.

Superstitions about Growth

Many of the traditional ceremonies and rituals which punctuate the life of the Zulu are commonplace and well-known, but in addition there are firmly-rooted practices which are of significance for the tribesman but which are rarely understood or even noticed by the outsider. Many of these practices are based on superstition or belief in magic and all are perpetuated from generation to generation.

One such practice relates to the way in which a parent or anyone else for that matter, would indicate the height of a specific child under discussion. The tribesman will never do so in the same way as a white man would; namely by putting out a flat hand with the palm towards the ground. That would be unlucky and would retard a child's growth. Instead, he puts out a *cupped* hand almost reverently with fingers pointing *upwards* towards the sky to symbolise growth and the back of the hand towards the ground at the appropriate height level.

They carry this superstition a step further when they describe the height of a maize crop or a goat or of anything else that has life and breathes. Here they hold the *edge* of their hand towards the ground with the palm and back facing sideways to the right and left. If they show the size of a stone or other *inanimate* object which 'has no life' the hand is put out indifferently in the way most white people know, with the palm towards the ground 'because that doesn't matter, you can't retard or harm a stone'.

Path to Adulthood

In the course of growing up and through subsequent adult life too, Zulu males and females graduate through a series of well-defined stages of seniority, each with its own complexities. If I were to deal with the many intricacies inherent in the system of social evolution of the Zulu, this book would become unnecessarily long and technical. With this in mind, I will touch briefly on only a few of the major milestones in their lives such as puberty, betrothal and marriage.

Custom Variations

I must emphasise that while the basic principles involved in Zulu customs have remained constant and differ very little throughout the nation, there are at times variations in the procedures in putting these customs into practice. The differences are usually localised and vary from clan to clan. This is because they stem mainly from practical needs or have come about for reasons of expedience. For instance a particular clan might not have a certain commodity in their area which is normally used for a certain rite. So they use a substitute. In due course that substitute becomes accepted as the norm. At other times, a chief may allow his followers to vary a long standing procedure to meet a necessity in particular circumstances and in time this revised procedure becomes the standard practice of his people and so on.

Among the Zulu of Natal to the south of the Tugela River and the original Zululand – particularly in the down-coast area towards Transkei – the influence of the neighbouring Xhosa is often apparent.

My idea in making these points is to illustrate why particular customs in recent years may have undergone some change among the Zulu. One particular custom which has lost a lot of its punch is the *physical* performance involved in a boy's puberty ceremony. More details are given later about this, but it can be said here that in the old traditional form of the ceremony, the procedures were conducive to boys becoming badly hurt and so most chiefs cut out the more rigorous parts and modified the ritual. The ritual of the puberty ceremony even though it may not be as vigorous as of old, still has deep spiritual significance.

Another old practice which is fading out is that of wearing earplugs, but the actual rite of puncturing the ears has not lost its symbolic religious importance.

Significance of Pierced Ears

I have mentioned that a Zulu man's (and woman's for that matter) life is divided into a series of stages of seniority. It is almost as if he has to climb a ladder from his mother's arms through to the ultimate ranks of a senior and respected elder and then eventually into the exalted region of his ancestral spirits.

Implicit faith in the existence of the spiritual world and in the power of its inhabitants over their living descendants explains much that is typical of the Zulu like their stoicism in the face of death, and their strength on their encounter with sorrow and hardship. I believe that they are helped at these times by their unqualified acceptance of the existence of the spiritual world and of the interest of their forefathers' in their affairs.

The first important rung a young Zulu climbs is at an age just before he reaches puberty. Traditionally at this time he has his ear lobes pierced to initiate him, or her, into the first stage of adulthood. The significance of this practice is that with the child reaching maturity he will have his ears 'opened' so that he may hear well and listen to the things of the world around him and understand them!

Only a few years ago the Zulu were conspicuous by their colourful ear decorations of painted wood or clay or even of cowhorn snuff boxes which they put into the slits of their earlobes. Not many of these are seen nowadays, although I have encountered some attractive specimens of ear decorations in clans like the *Cunu* in the quiet Tugela Ferry area, and the *Ntombela* further north in the rugged Mangeni hills near Isandlwana where in 1879 the Zulu warriors inflicted a crushing defeat in battle on the British Redcoats.

In his *The Zulu People*, A. T. Bryant gives a most expressive definition of the Zulu practice of 'boring' ears. He writes: 'A person with ears unbored was ridiculed as an *isi Cute* (a deaf person, one with ears unopened), or as an uncouth rustic (*o'Dlela em Kombeni we Mpaka*), or one-who-eats-out-of-the-trough-of-the-wild-cat'.

The need for astuteness in their senses is of particular importance to the tribespeople, and though I do not suggest that piercing of lobes improves their hearing, I do believe that the action illustrates their consciousness of the need for sharp senses in their kind of world. In their hunting days in the past, the faraway sound of an animal might have meant another day's food for them. Even today the call of a honeybird may lead the man of the hills to a cache of honey.

I had an experience in my own home in Pretoria, far away from the land of the kraals, which reminds me of how the Zulu and other black people use their trained senses in everyday life. It concerns Nozingozi, our urbanised Zulu housemaid. When she first joined us, my wife schooled her in her duties as cook and also showed her how to lay our table for meals. Among other things she was told she should always put a small handbell on the table. She did so once or twice, then stopped. My wife reminded her about it and for a day or two the bell was there and then it disappeared again. But the strange fact about it was that we did not actually need the bell to summon Nozingozi – she came in right on cue to clear the dishes each time we finished a course.

I was probably the first to notice this phenomenon and began to look for the explanation. I found it at breakfast one morning by analysing each of my own movements. I found that while I ate my porridge I kept my spoon in my hand, but at the end I put it down – I thought gently – in the plate. The 'clink' it made was adequate. It was her signal to bring in my bacon and eggs. Since then we have not called for the bell again because apart from a few rare occasions when we have wanted something out of the ordinary there has been no need to do so.

The 'Ear Surgeon'

I have already mentioned that the physical act of piercing the ear is part of the process of initiating the young Zulu into a higher status in life, but beyond that there are also deep religious and supernatural connotations attached to the ritual which do not belong in this book.

The operation of piercing or cutting the earlobes can be performed by either a male or a female, provided he or she is experienced in the art, does not suffer from wounds which will not heal and will not in any way contaminate the child. If the surgeon is a woman she must be past child-bearing age. The operator, however, has no concept of sterile conditions or the need for absolute physical cleanliness and uses any old instrument like a piece of iron picked up on a rubbish heap and sharpened to a razor-like edge, or an equally sharp, equally dirty, pocket-knife. While little attention is thus paid to physical hygiene for the operation strict precautions are taken to ensure that neither the surgeon nor the child, nor anyone else associated with the ritual, is 'unclean' through defilement in the spiritual sense at the time of the operation. For instance, the surgeon must not have had sexual contact for a day or two before the occasion, nor may anyone in the child's kraal have done so on the night before. Expectant mothers, similarly, are considered unclean and if the child has contact with such a person, he himself will become contaminated. His wounds will not heal and they will become swollen and ugly.

The operation itself is usually performed inside the gateway of the cattle-byre which is sacred ground frequented by the spirits. Blood from the wound must fall on the ground in the byre to consummate the rite. This, it seems, is part of the process of introducing the child to the ancestral spirits of the family and of establishing him as a member of that family itself.

If a child is nervous when the surgeon comes along with his sharp instrument, he is held fast by one or two assistants and is then allowed to scream as much as he likes. After the surgeon has punctured the ears he forces a piece of reed or a round stick into each hole to keep it open while the lobes heal. During this period the patient has to spin the plugs around occasionally to prevent them sticking. After this, progressively bigger reeds or discs replace the originals from time to time to stretch the lobes ever-wider and it is not unusual sometimes to see discs as big as four centimetres in diameter. The particular discs which the Zulu use when their ears are fully stretched vary according to the taste of the wearer. They may be snuff tins, specially painted discs of wood, or even rolls of brown paper. Often a person goes around with nothing in the hole at all and as he or she walks the great distended lobes hang free in a rather unsightly fashion and swing to and fro as the person moves.

In these times when someone does not intend to wear a disc, he simply has his ears punctured with a needle. Then the operator puts a strand of fibre or cotton through each hole and the patient moves it back and forth at intervals during the next few days until the wounds heal.

Puberty – Gateway to Manhood

Among many of Southern Africa's black people the gateway to final manhood is the circumcision rite. Among the Xhosa, for instance, it is the most important event in a man's life*. By contrast, this practice is extinct among the Zulu. The clan's of the Zulu nation practised circumcision in their early years, but by the beginning of the 1800's it was on its way out. Shaka finally put paid to the custom after he came to power in 1816 because it immobilised too many of his young warriors for months at a time when they should have been fighting for him. The Zulu of today regard the advent of puberty as the passport to adult status. It is a particularly important rung in the ladder of life, for both males and females alike. A boy at puberty is, in reality, little more than a child but in the Zulu world his acceptance into the ranks of men at that age has apparently not created any difficulty. The reason for this is, I think, that the Zulu's disciplinary codes are so entrenched and strictly adhered to that these young people know exactly where they stand and what is expected of them in their society, irrespective of whether they are called 'boys' or 'men'.

I have asked elderly Zulu men how they rate boys of puberty age and they say: 'They are men . . . but *young* men'. They also say that although such a man may mix in men's circles, he is expected to stay within his own age group and show respect for his elders. He is entitled to drink beer and in theory he could even marry, but in practice it would not be allowed.

This is a far cry from the old Shakan days when a youth had to go into one of Shaka's regiments and stay there until his whole regiment earned sufficient laurels to be permitted to marry and wear the headring which symbolised their superior status. Shaka frequently withheld this concession from a whole regiment until the average man in it was about thirty-five years old.

Boys' Puberty

In addition to the social significance of reaching puberty, the event is also important in a spiritual sense in that at this time the young man is introduced ritually to his ancestral spirits as a full member of his family and is commended to them for their blessing and protection so that he may journey well into the world ahead of him.

The status of a boy prior to puberty in so far as his own soul or spirit is concerned is not the same everywhere amongst the Nguni people, and if we go south to the Xhosa we find that they believe that young males are only united with their souls at their circumcision ceremony in their late teens. Prior to this they are just 'things'. In fact the Xhosa have a saying that 'boys are dogs'.

In some southern areas of Zululand the same view is held, albeit not quite so dogmatically. But the Zulu to the north have quite a different view. Senior men amongst them whom I have questioned insisted that boys are regarded as ordinary, normal people.

Irrespective of these divergent views, however, it seems that there is a definite intention in the puberty ceremony *(thomba)* to reinforce the boy as a person and bring him one link closer to his ancestral spirits. The religious side

The Magic World of the Xhosa

142

of the puberty ceremony is the most important part of it; the participant is doctored with various kinds of medicine, he has taboos placed on his foods and is kept completely away from any 'unclean' people. Finally he is presented to the ancestral spirits by being seated for the first and last time in his life, in the sacred *msamo* at the back of his father's 'big house'.

Whilst the religious significance of reaching the age of puberty has probably not diminished, the actual physical participation in the ceremony has. I have found that many young Zulu men of today are quite ignorant on this subject.

In some clans, nevertheless, old veterans die hard and I was fortunate to find one orthodox family whose head proudly told me that he would arrange for his young people to show me eaxctly how the ceremony is performed. He explained that the ritual starts with the first concrete evidence that the boy has reached puberty which is his first nocutral emission.

The night this happens the boy, having been primed in advance by his elders, gets up before dawn without waking anyone and steathily opens the gate of his father's cattle byre and 'steals' his cattle. The boys then demonstrated to me how a boy would drive the cattle out into the veld and up 'into the mountains'. There are, of course, parts of KwaZulu where there are not any mountains available so in reality the word is used in a figurative sense to imply a place where it would be difficult to find them. The idea is that the father then has to retrieve his cattle from the 'new man' who, with his new-gained strength, wishes to be regarded as an opposition to be reckoned with.

When the initiate's father discovers his son's disappearance, he loudly announces the news to everyone around and begins to prepare special medicines to doctor his son in accordance with the puberty ritual.

Meanwhile the news will also have spread amongst the boy's contemporaries who then 'steal' cattle from their fathers and drive them up into the mountain to join the initiate's herd. In different clans there are some diversities in the procedure followed to 'recover' the 'stolen' cattle. In the instance I witnessed there was a good deal of rough play in the form of stick-fighting and this, I believe, is one of the reasons why the physical aspect of the ceremony has been banned by some clan chiefs.

According to custom, the first move to get the stock back is to send the *girls* of the local kraals out with sticks and shields to fight the boys – who are armed in the same way – and recover them. Traditionally the girls used whipping switches but those I watched were experts at fighting with good heavy sticks.

I saw the two sides clash and some of the girls, who were no lightweights, flew at the boys like wild cats. The boys for their part treated them as such. It was breathtaking to see the vigour and vitality of these young people. Both boys and girls were highly skilled in the way they wielded their weapons and protected themselves with their shields. Sticks crashed against the hard leather shields with a tremendous clatter. But the girls could not keep up the pace for long. Female-like, one of them dropped her defences and stood where she was, giggling helplessly. She infected the rest and in a few moments they all broke and ran screaming and laughing homewards. The boys acclaimed themselves as heroes and helped them on their way. If the girls win – which is not impossible – the initiate-boy is branded a weakling.

The next attempt to recover the cattle was made by the men of the kraals. This was an awesome sight of the 'big guns' coming into play. It was devastating. The power of the men was frightening. They took no more than five minutes to send the youths scattering in all directions, even though some of them were already well built, sturdy young men.

Serious casualties can occur on these occasions and one man from the Nkwaleni valley whom I asked what they did about wounds said that if the cuts were open and bleeding, someone would simply take up a handful of earth and plug the wound to stem the flow of blood. If that did not work, the wound would be covered with the bark of a certain tree with medicinal qualities and then would be bound up with rushes or some other suitable material.

After this test of strength between fathers and sons, the cattle were gathered up and the young initiate was solemnly brought back to his father's kraal, walking in their midst into the home byre. Certain medicines were administered to him and then the cattle were again chased out of the kraal into the veld and left there. Then the beer drinking began with strict observance of the rules of etiquette and protocol.

In subsequent stages of this ritual, the boy is subjected to further doctoring with special medicines and is given instruction in kraal etiquette and on how to conduct himself as an adult. This process may last several days and the instruction received is taken very seriously by the initiate as the future pattern of behaviour for his adult life.

Girl's Puberty

A Zulu girl's puberty ceremony today is relatively simple in comparison with the complicated rituals followed in earlier times. Simplification of the procedures can be ascribed largely to economic factors because in modern times few fathers of marriageable daughters would at present-day prices be able to afford the animals which should be slaughtered at different stages of the ritual, nor perhaps would the daughters be happy to spend as much time in isolation as was originally prescribed by tradition.

Nevertheless, the modern version of this age-old custom still demands basic adherence to certain of the old rules relating to the 'coming out' of young girls. When a young girl first becomes aware of the physiological fact that she has reached the age of puberty and has her first menstruation she knows exactly what to expect because she will have been well instructed in this subject by her elder sisters and her mother. She knows that she must retreat behind a reed curtain which will be hung in her mother's hut to screen off a small area which is called the *mgonqo*. She remains isolated there for seven days and is fed on special herbal preparations by her mother to strengthen her. Her mother also sits inside the hut at the left of the entrance to attend to her needs. If she has, of necessity, to go out for personal reasons then she covers herself from head to foot so as not to be 'seen' and her mother, or a young female attendant, accompanies her. In the past, the initiate-girl used to have a number of friends of her own age attend her as well, but except in occasional highly orthodox families this does not appear to be a marked feature of the ritual anymore.

As in many Zulu rituals, the girl concerned is immediately subjected to the taboo of abstaining from sour milk or *amasi* which is an important part of the Zulu diet. This taboo is not lifted until the eighth day when her father formally frees her from it in what is called the *kwemula* rite. The word *kwemula* here means 'to start anew' or, more literally, 'to return to sour milk'. At this time, of course, she also emerges from her seclusion in the *mgonqo*. In the olden days animals were slaughtered for her at this time to free her from contamination but this cleansing is now embodied in the simplified form of the rite. The *amasi*

GROWING UP

From an early age little Zulu girls act as nursemaids to the babies of the neighbourhood.

A child anywhere . . .

As they sit beside an underground grain storage pit which was opened for the first time earlier in the day, these two young ladies consider whether the poison gases have yet dispersed.

Referee's 'warbling' whistles are always popular with dancers.

Beadwork

148

This drum has hide on one side only with a smooth round rod fastened into it and extending out the opposite side. The drummer pulls wet hands along it towards herself to produce a low penetrating drone. An assistant sits on the drum to keep it steady.

Young Zulu men are always extremely fit but their dances are vigorous and demand periodic breaks.

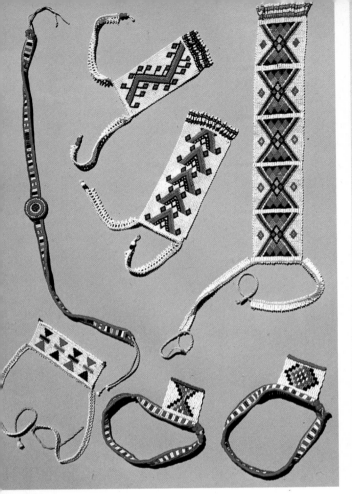

Geometrical designs are used a great deal in beadwork.

A maiden's skirt or apron in a clan in the south of Natal.

Caterpillar cocoons filled with tiny pebbles to form rattles are popular for dancing or jogging and are used extensively not only by the Zulu but also by the Xhosa and other tribes in Southern Africa.

Girls do all their own beadwork
and also that worn by their
boy-friends. Married men wear
few, if any, beads.

A girl of the Shembe *Christian*
religion. These girls sometimes
wear a greater weight and volume
of beads than girls in any other
part of KwaZulu.

An old "smithy" has a chat with a little friend before getting down to work.

The drummer and the dancers

A young man's hairstyle I found among the Tembu in the Tugela Ferry area. Both males and females have their ears punctured and wear discs of the type seen here in their distended lobes.

Typical back aprons worn by little girls in some areas.

When a girl becomes engaged to be married, her father instructs her to grow her hair and put it up in the style of a married woman and to don the leather skirt of a woman to show her status publicly.

The first step in a boy's puberty rite. He 'steals' his father's cattle in the night or early dawn and takes them to 'the mountains'.

There, his contemporaries join him and they prepare to resist those who wish to re-capture the cattle.

The girls come out to fight the adolescents in the hope of re-capturing the 'stolen' cattle.

If the girls are defeated, the adult men come out and conquer the boys and take them and the cattle back home where the puberty rite enters its next stage.

Boy and girl friend.

taboo connected with menstruation is still rigidly applied and it appears to have had its origins far back in the mists of time but there seems to be little, if any, common knowledge as to the specific era or civilisation in which it originated.

Permission to Marry

After emerging from her first *kwemula* the girl returns to normal everyday life with a few additional liberties and privileges until, in due course, she reaches the stage where she begins to think of marriage. Marriage for the Zulu girl is not something she can enter into lightly or even of her own accord. It is a giant step up the ladder for her and an event in which her father plays a major role in that he has to give his public consent, firstly for her to enter the marriage field and thereafter for her to marry the particular man she chooses.

The people of the country kraals usually do not know their own age in years because they are largely illiterate, so a maiden's fitness for marriage is judged mostly on her physical development and maturity. In addition, the seniority of her contemporary age-group in the kraals is a lead which enables her father to decide if she is old enough to marry.

Sometimes, in spite of her age, her father is slow to make the first move in proclaiming that his daughter is officially eligible for serious courtship with a view to marriage. He might know that she has been given permission by the senior guild of girls to *hlobonga* (have external intercourse), but is secretly reluctant to let her leave home while he and his wife can still keep her. In these cases the daughter stirs him into action with a formula prescribed specially for use by Zulu girls on such occasions. She suddenly refuses to eat sour milk (*amasi*) without having any physical reason to abstain or observe such a taboo. He does not lightly ignore such a tacit request from his daughter and usually reacts in the right way.

In prosperous families, who are also strong traditionalists, the father even today often follows an old custom of giving her a major *kwemula* ceremony which could be likened to a 'coming out'.

The Kwemula Rite

The rite begins with the girl going into isolation in the *mgonqo* (partitioned-off area) in a hut at her home kraal for about three months with the idea of making her fat and beautiful in preparation for the ultimate marriage. In this period her every whim, especially in the food category, is attended to and she has merely to suggest that she would like a tin of condensed milk, for instance, and her little hand-maiden or *phini* will be sent to the trading store to fetch one, or she may say that she is 'hungry for goat's meat' and her father will slaughter a goat for her. She fills out enormously to become the admiration of all because slim, trim, figures are not for the Zulu. They regard a girl with fine firm breasts as a child. In fact breasts are hardly rated as a feature of beauty at all and are of relatively little interest in the eyes of men, but well-developed buttocks count for high marks.

At a dance which I once saw to celebrate a girl's coming out of isolation, the debutante emerged particularly fat. A girl in the crowd who could speak English looked at her with tremendous admiration. She held up her little finger and said, 'You know when she went into her hut three months ago, she was as thin as this!' That typified the opinion of most of those present of just how successful the girl's stay in isolation had been and how lucky the man would be who won her heart.

The full ceremony is a costly affair and it seems that today even a wealthy father can afford to put only his first-born daughter through the 'coming out' ritual. On rare occasions this privilege may be extended to the youngest daughter in the family as well, but never to those between. Accordingly any girl who has been through this impressive ceremony gathers a certain amount of personal prestige and so does her father because he has proved beyond doubt that he is a successful man who can afford not only the luxuries his daughter demanded during her seclusion, but the large *cece* party at her coming out.

Cece Dance

The *cece* dance is the final act in a girl's major *kwemula* rite. It constitutes the forum from which her father publicly signifies his acceptance of the fact that she has reached marriageable age and may be courted. I have watched these 'coming out' dances several times and they vary little in procedure, but the scene on the first occasion made such an impact on me that it remains vividly in my mind to this day.

When I arrived at the large open space where the ceremony was to be held, an ox had already been slaughtered and large quantities of home-made sorghum beer brewed. Still more was continuously being brought in by the guests. The debutante, they said, was still down at the river washing, but in due course she arrived with her retinue of about thirty girls and was conspicuous not only by her substantially greater weight, but by the fact that over her otherwise naked torso she wore the customary 'shawl' of the caul of the ox slaughtered on her behalf for the spirits of her ancestral fathers. It covered her ample bosom and hung halfway down her back.

From a distance the fatty substance with its fine tracery of red blood vessels, looked almost like a pattern in lace.

The troupe of girls formed up in a row for their dance. The debutante herself, and two girls on each side of her, carried an assegai in their right hands. Ahead of them, across an open space, sat silent rows of senior men quietly smoking and drinking beer from black clay pots. The girls all wore tight black hair-nets on their heads (another modern innovation) and in addition the debutante's hair was adorned with rows of large safety pins about which I learned more later.

The dance started slowly and monotonously in serious mood. The girls swayed back and forth and shuffled their feet almost aimlessly. Then, when I least expected anything, two elderly women from the crowd rushed out onto the field ululating in high-pitched voices. They carried small green branches in their hands and ran all over the field 'sweeping away' evil influences.

After this, the girls warmed up their tempo a little and I saw the five girls with their assegais come out ahead of the row. Their pace quickened, their bodies swayed and they began to brandish their assegais in the air. Then they lifted their heads and I saw them each obviously 'fix' on a man. They opened out in different directions and each girl danced briskly up to the man of her choice and plunged her assegai into the ground in front of him where she left it standing upright, quivering at his feet.

In perfect orderliness each danced back to unite with the other four. They reformed their rank and moved back rythmically to join the team. The men outwardly ignored the incident and sipped away at their beer without any comment. Five minutes later the eldest of them leapt to his feet, tore the assegai from the ground and cavorted around stabbing it in all directions at imaginery enemies. He was as nimble as any teenage warrior.

Then he set his sights on the debutante. With the spear held high above his head in a threatening throwing position, he raced across the field at her, leaping and posturing as he went. He stopped abruptly in front of her and viciously jabbed the spear into the ground at her feet. He fumbled in the back pocket of his white-man style trousers (probably bought specially for this occasion) and brought out a crisp green bank note. Everyone gasped. It was all of ten rand. The girl bent her head graciously forward and with excited, trembling fingers, he opened a safety pin in her hair and firmly impaled the note in it without removing it from her head. The crowd applauded loudly in appreciation of the old man's generous gift as he went quietly and soberly back to his beer pot. There were still four spears standing in the ground in front of the other selected men who, one by one, sprang to their feet and repeated the old man's performance. None had the money to equal his gift, but with warm hearts each pinned his donation to the lucky lady's hair. Later, the girls again chose another five men, then another and another, until at the end of the day, the debutante's head was a colourful mass of banknotes, fluttering in the afternoon breeze.

I heard later that her harvest that afternoon was one hundred and fifty Rand, which is a reasonable amount for any potential bride to spend on items for her trousseau. After this, her 'big *kwemula*', a girl still might not marry for some time, but in the meanwhile she is in no way barred from participating in the normal fun of the kraal.

Formative Years

Like young people everywhere, Zulu boys and girls enjoy each other's company. They enjoy life. It is spent largely in the open and it is free and simple but it is disciplined where discipline is necessary in the interests of their society. We know, for instance, that senior boys and girls are allowed to spend nights together, alone and naked, in the *hlobonga* hut but custom demands that she must still ultimately go to her bridegroom a virgin.

My use of the word 'boys' in the last paragraph is purely to differentiate between them and more senior men because, in theory, a male is a man after puberty albeit a 'little man'. The teenage years of the young Zulu are vital formative years because even though the young man may be wild, reckless and rough during them, he has certain barriers beyond which he may not go. His father drills him in tribal codes of honour so that he does not bring shame to his parents or disgrace to his kraal. A father goes even further than this, in that he schools his son in how to take care of himself and of a family so that he can ultimately take his place with dignity in the community and in the clan.

In their homeland hills the young men help their fathers in the male duties of the kraal and relieve them of many of their more arduous tasks. With the advance of modern civilisation, many go out into the world to Natal's sugar cane or other industries and further afield still to the cities and become increasingly Westernised. Despite the bright lights of the outside world, however there are few things that a tribesman away from home cherishes more than a periodic return to his old home kraal.

Sport

A major form of entertainment among young Zulu men is stick-fighting in which they either match each other singly or in groups. The fighters carry a shield made of ox-hide in their left hand to parry opposition blows, and a good strong stick – about 90 cm. or three feet long – in their right. They attack with this and their target is usually the other man's skull, although in a fight they use all their skill to strike a blow that hurts anywhere on the body. The sportsmen are often injured badly, but the dexterity with which a good fighter defends himself and the personal agility and strength he has to draw on in counter attack often saves him from worse trouble.

Another form of relaxation among the young people, this time of both sexes, is dancing. When and wherever a group of young people find themselves together they inevitably end up dancing, no matter what time of the day or night. Preparations are unnecessary although ceremonies and feasts are also automatically venues for a dance – usually in the open veld. While the white man's style of dress is encroaching into most Zulu areas, the dress at ceremonies in the more isolated places is often largely orthodox Zulu, with the boys in fur aprons and cow-tail arm and leg bands and the girls bare-topped but otherwise laden with colourful beadwork.

It is almost impossible to define the Zulu dancing specifically because it varies according to the occasion and is modified to suit events. Males and females do not dance together as partners although they do sometimes form up in rows opposite each other and gyrate, clap their hands to body movements and stamp their feet; but they just as easily separate and dance, each with their own sex.

Dance of the Warriors One of the most dramatic dancing sessions I have watched was one evening by firelight when Kingsley Holgate organised a group of local Zulu to dance in his specially prepared open-air setting. The flames of a great wood fire were between me and a dozen splendidly-built young men in warriors plumes and white cowtail arm-and-leg decorations, dancing in a row. The bright glow from the fire outlined every muscle of their lithe bodies which began to glisten with perspiration as the dance progressed. Their shields were white and black with plumes of white at the top. All of them carried knobkerries except their leader who had an assegai.

One particularly interesting dance was one which started with a group of girls singing a lively song called 'catch the dance, its running away'. Then, with fine, strong resonant voices, the young men joined in and simultaneously leapt bare-footed into the arena with its well-trodden earth floor. Their timing took them straight into the rhythm of the dance with free and easy body movements. Then the clapping of the girls increased in tempo and so did the dance until it built up to a tremendous crescendo. Then, excitedly, the married women from the crowd rose to their feet and added their clapping to the accompaniment. At the same time they began to dance in little groups of their own.

Suddenly, at a signal from their leader, the male troupe dropped like one man to the ground and sat motionless cross-legged with their shields held end-to-end in a barrier in front of them. A glowing log in the fire broke, and as it settled threw up a fan of flames which for a few moments lit up the scene of a dozen warriors poised like granite statues, unflinching and unmoving. The whites of their plumes and shields shone gold in the light and it was as if the Great Artist had created this picturesque scene just to show the beauty waiting in all places and in all things for those to see who can appreciate them.

A moment later the men dropped their guard, relaxed and wiping the perspiration from their brows with their curved forefingers, flicked it off into the dust. Their rest was of short duration and was broken by the boom of a drum which came like thunder out of the darkness behind them. A second drum followed, then a third. The troupe tensed, moved to the alert on their haunches and waited for their cue. Then came a piercing war cry and the men were on their feet.

The drums began again like the return of a storm and the dancers picked up their beat and began to dance. It was probably a dance which their grandfathers did long before them. In splendid unison they brought their knees up almost to their chins and stamped their feet on the ground with a thud which made me flinch. Time and time again they repeated this in the process of their different movements. At the same time they went through other equally vigorous actions. The vitality they displayed and the power they put into every stamp left me speechless. For this dance there was no hand-clapping in accompaniment – only the great throb of the drums. Great throbs which rolled away far into the valleys and echoed back from the hills.

The dancers *lived* their part and saw nothing save a scene in their imaginations – for this was their interpretation of a war dance by Shaka's warriors of old.

Chapter 7
Courtship and Marriage

After ceremonies and feasts young men and senior girls often pair off together and disappear into the dark to spend the night together. This is a custom condoned by parents. In fact, the mothers of the girls sometimes encourage such 'get togethers' but fathers pretend they know nothing about what is going on.

Although the young have these liberties, full sex among them is taboo and they have to discipline themselves to the practice of *hlobonga* or external sex only. The tribespeople have no inhibitions in discussing intimate subjects like this and when a girl is considered old enough to have a regular boy-friend, she is told by the senior girls or by her mother how to handle the situation and is instructed in the art of lying on her right side on her garments or on a blanket without letting herself get into a compromising situation.

The preservation of a girl's virginity is safeguarded by the principle of limited sex only but evidence which I have found seems to suggest that morals are now tending to weaken in this respect. One old Zulu man summed up his views for me in a few simple words when he said: 'Young people these days are getting very naughty – especially when they live away from the kraals!'

Girls' Guilds

After puberty girls advance through several 'guilds' or groups until they reach the most senior grade which is that of being eligible for marriage. The girls in this class play an important role in kraal life because to them is allocated the task and responsibility of governing the younger girls and guiding them in their love affairs. It is their duty to teach the young girls how to conduct themselves with members of the opposite sex and *their* initial approval of a girl's chosen boy-friend or lover is essential in a young love affair. In some instances, the authority of senior girls over their juniors and even over some of those of their own contemporaries actually takes the place of parental authority. Sometimes in a senior guild one member is elected queen or leader, but the chosen girl is not always happy to accept this honour because the belief is still held among many Zulu that this is an unlucky position and that when the incumbent eventually marries, her children will die.

The Love Affair

When Zulu boy meets Zulu girl and hearts begin to warm, there are certain formalities and rules of etiquette to be observed before the two can set foot on the path that will lead them ultimately to marriage. Firstly, it depends on whether the senior girls have decided that the young girl has reached the stage where she may have a steady boy-friend, and permission must then be obtained from them rather than from the girl's parents to start their courtship. The senior girls will also decide whether the girl may accept an engagement proposal from a specific young man and at what stage the couple may begin to indulge in the privileges associated with their closer relationship, such as *hlobonga*. But even before that, the young man has to observe the etiquette demanded of would-be lovers and follow the prescribed ritual of extracting a confession from his sweetheart of *her* love for him. This is a strange procedure, yet one which is insisted upon in the customs of the kraals.

In 'proposing' the young man does not make an outright suggestion of his love or even mention the subject. Instead he awaits an opportune moment when he is alone with the lady of his choice to badger her with questions – about anything – and to tease her until eventually he provokes her into answering.

Having been taught to expect this sort of behaviour from a would-be lover, she resists as long as she can. 'Sometimes all day,' one Zulu told me. The more she ignores him the more he talks, acts and teases. Having had no response from her in all this time, he now decides on the next step which is to 'open her mouth'. He takes her a present for this purpose. Just a simple present like a small rainbow-coloured bangle of celluloid from the trader.

If she has no affection for him he will have known from her early reactions and abandoned his quest, but by the same token, he senses from her warmth when she approves of him. In the latter case, when she gets her gift, she still may not say 'yes' outright but instead agrees to consult the girls of the senior guild. The chances are that they or their 'queen' will give permission, but if they have a good reason such as the young man being 'one who is lazy and never works' they may refuse to allow a courtship.

The parents of the girl at this stage are not told of what is, in reality, their daughter's formal engagement by which she has signified her willingness to go through to ultimate marriage to the man. Sometimes they discreetly hide what perhaps they do know.

After the lapse of a specified time of courtship, the senior guild grant permission for the practice of *hlobonga*. The girl may then spend nights out with her sweetheart, but must always be back home before sunrise otherwise her lover has to pay her father a penalty of a goat.

These are basic principles involved in courtship, but in particularly orthodox societies the technicalities are often more detailed and intricate than this, and sometimes may even vary somewhat in different areas.

For instance, I was told in the *Nkandla* area that when a girl with several suitors decides which one of them she likes best, she takes a long white bead necklace and places it around his neck to show that she has chosen him. Then the others will not worry her further.

Changing times are diluting many old customs like these, and sad to say not always for the best. Breaks from old understood traditions which have been anchors of their society for generations can take away a sense of stability without necessarily putting anything the people can understand in its place.

Exogamy

Perhaps one of the least flexible of the Zulu laws governing young people who wish ultimately to marry is the law on exogamy which prohibits intermarriage between members of the same clan. Because a clan is in fact regarded as one large family, a member of the *Biyela* clan, for instance, may not marry another *Biyela* or an *Ntuli* marry another *Ntuli* no matter how far back the original family link was or whether it can even be traced at all.

In real life all the boys and girls of contemporary age belonging to the same clan regard each other as brothers and sisters and all the joint *parents* are their parents. They are called 'father' and 'mother' as readily as are those who bore them. If as an example anyone with the name of Ntuli should find himself at another Ntuli kraal no matter where, he is welcomed without reservation and brought in and given the freedom of the home, 'his home'. He is never treated as a stranger even if he is completely unknown.

While the origin of this law of exogony may not have been traced, it is not difficult, in view of clansmans' attitude towards each other, to appreciate why the law is so strict. The clan relationship is naturally a major factor in binding clansmen together as a unit.

The Courting Hut

In love affairs as in so many aspects of kraal life, there are customs and practices which are fascinating because of their subtlety and the devious manner in which they are executed. The art of courting comes into this category. Here, even though father feigns ignorance of the love affairs of his daughters and will not allow their boy-friends to be seen at his home, he nevertheless builds a special courting hut within his own kraal for them. He places it discreetly next to a private gateway where the boys can come and go inconspicuously so that 'he-knows-but-he-doesn't-know' what goes on. It is a *hlobonga* hut.

Engagement Procedures

Early on in a courtship a girl inevitably confides in her mother, and apart from this the news filters through to her friends. But father still feigns ignorance; that is, until he thinks the time is ripe. Then, if the young man has not yet sent an emissary to ask for the girl's hand, her father bluntly tells her to 'go and fetch some cattle' from her lover. Such a statement, in effect, is her father's formal expression of his approval of his daughter's engagement and his suggestion that it is time the young man began *lobolo* negotiations with him. Even before this the girls of the senior guild pay a visit to the would-be bridegroom's kraal to satisfy themselves that it is a fitting home for their 'sister'. Likewise, the would-be bridegroom's 'mothers'* also pay a courtesy visit to the future bride's mother. These and many other similar formalities which are observed in the pre-marriage and the marriage rites are often delightful in their degree of refinement. It is also customary now for the bride-to-be to pay secret visits to her lover at his home and sleep with him in his hut. But they still have to remember the *hlobonga* rule!

The father of the potential bride does not usually take the initiative in setting marriage arrangements in motion except when he fears that his daughter is not likely otherwise to find a husband. Normally the first move comes from the young man's kraal when they send an emissary to the girl's father to discuss the *lobolo* terms with him. When the emissary arrives, the father stages an almost routine act. He pretends to be indignant and denies that he even has a daughter of marriageable age and sometimes he even refuses to discuss the visitors ridiculous suggestions. Then the emissary will probably go back to his home kraal and fetch a present of an ox to 'open the father's teeth' to get him to speak!

Lobolo Negotiations

In the present times 'ten plus one' head of cattle is the *lobolo* figure for a virgin. The 'one' is to compensate her mother for the sadness of losing a daughter and the 'ten' cattle are for her father. The number of cattle asked for a chief's daughter may be as much as forty or more. If a bride-to-be is no longer a virgin, the number is reduced by one, and if she has children her father loses one for each child she has borne. The *lobolo* for a widow is less than for a girl and is

*His literal's mother and her co-wives.

168

usually by arrangement. In her case the cattle are given to her eldest Right-Hand* son as her late husband's automatic heir. He is entitled to them by virtue of the fact that on his father's death he became head of the home and custodian of all its inhabitants, including his own mother.

Zulu men marry relatively young – usually in their early twenties – and at that age they seldom have the means to pay *lobolo* and so their fathers and older brothers have to assist them to find the wherewithal. Cattle are paid in advance to the girl's father and usually in instalments over a protracted period. Sometimes after about eight head of cattle out of the stipulated total of ten plus one have been delivered, he allows the marriage to take place. At other times he may also accept partial payment in goats and/or cash if the bride's family cannot meet the full commitment in cattle. Another old Zulu custom which is still sometimes practised where a young man has difficulty in raising *lobolo* cattle, is for him to pledge to his wife's father and mother, in lieu of cattle, his first-born daughter, even before she is born. In such a case the child is brought up by its parents but when she starts to develop physically in her teenage years, she actually goes to live with her grandparents who in due course marry her off as their own daughter. Grandfather claims the *lobolo* for her in the place of that which she should originally have received for his own daughter.

But we must return to the subject of *lobolo* and other aspects of the engagement or betrothal procedures which we left at the stage where the girl's father comes into the open and tacitly gives his approval of his daughter's romance by telling her to fetch cattle from her lover.

Once a father formally recognises his daughter's engagement, then important developments take place in the courtship sequence. First, her father instructs her to prepare her hair so that when it has grown sufficiently it can be put up into the high style used by married women. She also has to discard her girl's skirt and don the leatherpleated skirt or *sidwaba* of a woman. In this way her new status as a formally engaged girl is publicised for all to see. One of her first actions after this is to present herself, with another girl of the senior guild, at the 'great house' of her husband-to-be's parents where many niceties such as the exchange of gifts between the parties and other acts of *hlonipha* are observed by her and by her future in-laws.

If practical a goat is killed for her but she may not eat of its meat because it is taboo to her. Others eat it all and the young people of the kraal turn out in full force and indulge in hours of jubilant dancing and feasting to show their pleasure.

This constitutes a formal announcement of the girl's engagement.

Meanwhile at the bride's home, her parents are sad at the prospect of losing their daughter, but at the same time the mother is not averse to subtly turning the situation to her own advantage..I found a delightful example of this refined form of extortion among the *Cele* tribe in the south of Natal. Here the mother of an engaged girl tells the father that she (the mother) is 'cold' because she has not got a daughter any more! Father then has to go off to the trader to buy her some tea and sugar and spoons and a cup to 'warm her again'.

| *The White Flag and*
the Red | The bridegroom-elect now sets out to publicise his engagement to all and sundry. To do this he plants the tallest pole he can find, which is usually a |

---

*This is explained later in this chapter.

bamboo at least six metres high, in front of his home with a white flag fluttering at the top. The higher the flag the happier the man, the Zulu say. This custom is common throughout Zulu country but I once encountered something far more unusual, deep in the rugged hills north-east of the mediaeval Nkandla forest. It was a red flag fluttering boldly beside the white.

When I asked my Zulu companion what this meant, he told me that the white flag as usual, indicated that the man was engaged to be married, but that the red meant that at the same time he was looking further afield for yet another wife. 'The man is boasting,' my friend said, 'that he has good red blood, the colour of that flag!' It was obviously also a sign of his prosperity and wealth in cattle. The flag custom is practised not only by a young man taking his first wife but also by older married men who already have established kraals of their own.

Lobolo *Principles*

I have explained how the value of the *lobolo* to be paid in cattle or otherwise by the bridegroom for his bride is determined. Now I take this highly complex subject a little further to indicate broadly what some of the principles are on which the *lobolo* system is based.

Lobolo is variously described by laymen, but one definition which is used perhaps too lightly is that it is the 'price paid for a wife'. Students of tribal culture are strongly opposed to the contention that the cattle, in fact, represent a *price*. Instead, they argue that the *lobolo* cattle are *compensation* for the loss that the girl's father, her kraal and clan suffer and for the void she leaves when she is taken away by her husband to join his people and his clan.

From a less sentimental and more practical point of view, *lobolo* is also a settlement made to a bride's father to secure the rights of the bridegroom's family and his clan to any children born of the marriage. This is an important aspect of the *lobolo* custom because it has the added implication or assumption that the bride will, in fact, be able to bear children to perpetuate her husband's family line. This implied condition is apparent in the fact that if a wife proves barren, then her husband is entitled to claim at least the greater number of his cattle back and the father may even have to take his daughter back into his kraal. An alternative which is not uncommon is for the father to substitute another of his daughters for the barren wife. A further alternative is that the husband may elect that the barren girl should stay on as his wife but that her father should send her sister to 'put children into her womb'.

This simply means that the sister will bear children by the husband for the wife. For all practical purposes such children are then regarded and treated as if they actually were the natural children of the unsuccessful wife who retains her official status, and the children inherit the same rights as her own children would have done.

While no *lobolo* is given for the second daughter, the bridegroom is expected to take anything from one to three head of cattle to his father-in-law just to thank him!

Those who are accustomed to the tribesman's way of thinking and understand some of the intricacies of tribal culture, will appreciate the depth of reasoning in this philosophy even though there may be some modern fathers who with their more mercenary ideas, undoubtedly tarnish the image of the old system of *lobolo*.

There is little doubt that the *lobolo* system has decided benefits among the black people. It is a stabilising factor in that it makes marriage a highly organised system because no man can lightly, easily or without careful planning, take a wife. Nor can she easily leave him, for if she did her father would have to return the *lobolo*. Similarly, he cannot divorce her without the penalty of forfeiting the cattle. In what is certainly a man's world it gives a bride and wife a status and confidence in her own value. She sees tangible evidence of what she means to the man who seeks her as his wife and life companion by yielding up so many cattle for the benefit of sharing his life with her.

The Marriage Ceremony

After their formal engagement and once the terms of the *lobolo* have been settled between the two families, the advance delivery of instalments of cattle begins, but a date for the marriage is not normally fixed immediately. In practice a courtship may go on for a year or two, but now lovemaking by *hlobonga* is formally permitted. Even when the cattle have all been delivered to the bride-to-be's father, he frequently stalls her departure from home because he and his wife are loath to part with their daughter.

At the insistence of the young man and his family, a date for the wedding is ultimately decided upon and plans are made for the ceremony. In choosing the date care is always taken to ensure that the moon is not at its faintest at that time because the day which follows the darkest night is a 'black day' which is unlucky. In addition to this the guests like to have moonlit nights for their revelry of feasting, drinking and dancing which is carried on over several days mostly in the open air. Few kraals would be able to accommodate indoors all of the large crowd which invariably attends a wedding. The venue of the marriage ceremony is the bridegroom's home kraal, but the parents of the bride do not attend because the occasion would be too sad for them to bear.

On the appointed day the bride arrives with a retinue of bridesmaids all carrying parts of her trousseau on their heads. In some clans a decorative 'marriage box' is fashionable and this houses sundry of the bride's smaller items like her clothes and beadwork and bangles and baubles, but her sleeping mat and bigger items she carries separately. In addition to these items, wealthy fathers provide their daughters with many presents for her future in-laws. A trader once told me that it is not uncommon for him to sell two dozen blankets alone, apart from other gifts, to the father of the bride for this purpose.

As in most tribal ceremonies, the bride's ritual begins with a morning at the river where she and her handmaidens spend their time bathing naked. This process is largely symbolic of cleansing from impurity. Thereafter, at the wedding kraal, she works her way through two or three days of complex rites and rituals in which she partakes of sacred portions of meat or follows taboos and gives gifts and pays respect. She is subjected to many formalities which she goes through with precision and in a mood of serious dignity until, in the closing stages, she eventually carries her sleeping mat and other goods into her bridegroom's hut.

Marriage is an occasion to strengthen ties between two clans. This is done in a strange manner and in a way which in fact hardly sounds conducive to fostering good relations. But then, many things the tribespeople do are hardly designed to be understood by the outsider.

As the guests arrive, the people of the bridegroom's clan keep to themselves and do not associate with those of the bride. Instead the members of the two clans form up in lines which literally oppose each other. At this stage the attitude is always one of such rivalry and even hostility that the chiefs of the clans concerned know in advance what potential dangers lie in the situation and always send policemen or *maphoyisa* to a wedding to keep order and, as far as possible, prevent bloodshed.

As the excitement grows with the arrival of new guests to swell the numbers, the clans mock and taunt each other with insulting and challenging remarks. Each tries to outdo the other in its dancing and singing. Eventually fever pitch is reached when the *lobolo* cattle given for the bride are publicly paraded for the guests to see. When this happens, each animal is discussed in minute detail: the shape of its horns, how fat or thin it is, and everything about it which can give rise to comment, but no matter how attractive the cattle are, the bride's clan are unlikely to over-enthuse about them or praise them adequately. After all, hardly anything could be good enough as *lobolo* for someone from *their* clan.

Sometimes the taunting goes a little too far and fierce fights break out particularly between the young men and then the *phoyisa* have to take a firm hand and deal with the situation promptly before it gets out of control. With the progress of the wedding ceremony which usually lasts about three days, a phase is reached where the enmity between the two clans is formally cleared up by the slaughter of two head of cattle – one for each clan. Then an exchange of meat takes place between the clans, and by this token, the two clans become symbolically united. Thereafter the barriers are down and instead of drinking their beer separately, they unite and drink as one group and relations are cemented even further until ultimately the ceremony ends in the highest possible spirits, not only as a wedding between two people but as a unifying force between two clans.

The Life of a Bride   When a girl marries, she adopts her husband's clan or *isibongo* and while the couple may, because of circumstances related to their case, find it more convenient to build their home in a place of their own, it is more traditional for them to settle in the bridgroom's father's kraal. There they fall under the jurisdiction of the father as head of the household and greater family, and they must obey his dictates.

The bride's status at this stage is junior and humble and she treats her father-in-law with profound reverence and her mother-in-law with hardly less. Her husband too has to be shown respect and implicitly obeyed. Apart from a display of basic humility, she pays respect in specific ways according to *hlonipha* requirements. For instance, she wears a veil of beads or cloth well down over her eyes – one reason for which is that she may not 'look her father-in-law in the eyes' until she has proved herself by presenting him with a grandchild! She refrains from using many everyday Zulu words in her conversation and instead uses a special vocabulary of substitute words in their place. In particular she may not use a word which starts with the same letter of the alphabet as her father-in-law's or her husband's names because it would be presumptuous of her and disrespectful to do so. When she speaks to her husband in casual conversation, she must sit down and put her hands on her knees in front of her in respect. These are but a few of her *hlonipha* practices but there are many, many more.

For the first few days in her father-in-law's kraal she eats with the family so that she may have a short spell to settle in but after a few days her father-in-law surprises her by saying: 'You have got to cook today!' This means that it is time for her now to go back to her father and ask him for a cooking pot of her own.

This is a gift expected of him. Her father accordingly goes off to the nearest trader and buys her a present of a three-legged cast-iron pot for cooking over an open fire in the conventional way.

After this the bride has to do all the cooking for her parents-in-law. She gets up at dawn to light the fires and prepare their food in their kitchen. Sometimes she is allowed to cook for them at her own fire and then bring the food to their hut. She is, however, not allowed to enter the great hut but has to bring the food near to the door then go down on her knees and respectfully call out that she has arrived. One of the father's own children or even his wife collects the food from his daughter-in-law and takes it to him in his hut. If there are several married sons living with their wives at the same kraal, the young wives are jointly responsible for serving the family head in this way.

If at any time a bride is given a present by her family of, say, a fowl or a goat, then according to the custom of the kraals she and her husband may not simply kill it and eat it themselves at will. Instead, when it is cooked, she has to offer it to her father-in-law for the first picking and he takes whatever choice parts he likes and as much as he likes. After this she may take what is left back for her husband and herself.

A bride's domestic routine in her own home is largely one of hard work. She gathers the wood for the home fires and carries water; she hoes her husband's crops and cooks. Life, even though simple, is now rather more serious than her recently-shed adolescent years, but she accepts her position with quiet dignity and where before she flirted with her male friends and came and went largely as she pleased, now she is expected to be obedient and humble and to pay deep respect to one who was once a gay lover but has now become a stern master. Where previously she was a member of a senior guild dictating to younger girls, now she is a junior wife serving and obeying a new family. Although she will have climbed to the last rung in her ladder of girlhood, it is only to find that ahead of her lies a new set of steps patiently to be ascended. But the years take her up in their stride and carry her forward again and again until she, like those before her, ultimately becomes an elder among Zulu women.

Customs like these I have mentioned, are all part of the complex system of codes in the Zulu kraals and though many of their habits and ways may seem strange – and others perhaps tough – the Zulu understand them and like them and often shake their heads in bewilderment at some of the *white* man's 'peculiar' habits which they consider meaningless, weak or foolish. Be that as it may, there is one custom with which the Zulu man's white counterpart will never agree. It is that the Zulu do not kiss! 'Not even in lovemaking,' one old Zulu told me. In an attempt to satisfy myself on this point, I followed it up further with someone else who said: 'Kissing is for behind *closed* doors. It is not for others to see!' Either way, it is certainly not common practice, and the only Zulu people I have ever seen kiss are a mother and her baby.

Another facet of the love-scene which I find interesting is the routine followed by a husband returning home after a lengthy period of absence from his wife. He never goes straight back to her. Instead he deviates via his parents' home even if it means taking a different road. There he enquires how things are at his own home and asks if all is well in it. After that he goes to his wife, but when he arrives neither he nor his wife show any emotion. 'No smiles . . . they just look at each other!' But I have been told that if his heart is very warm and happy inside then he might just touch her on the shoulder and say 'I missed you!' That night he sleeps with her and only the *next* day (if all has gone well) they release their pent-up excitement and openly express their joy!

Polygamy

As a married man matures in life and prospers and gathers cattle of his own, it is likely that his mind will turn to the possibility of taking another wife or two.

While they are in the minority in relation to one-wife marriages, polygamous marriages are still common among the Zulu although there seems little doubt that the ratio between the two categories is changing, with one-wife marriages gaining a longer lead. Of the polygamous marriages that do occur, fewer men appear to be taking more than two or three wives. A man with four or six wives falls into the 'rare' class. These are my own opinions based on enquiries of a purely general nature. Among the kraal people I would suggest that polygamous marriages are not less popular today – in fact such a marriage is regarded as a status symbol for a man – but the continually increasing costs of finding sufficient *lobolo* cattle and then of having to support large families is mitigating against the practice. In addition to his wives he is also permitted to have an unmarried 'sweetheart' with whom he may spend the night but this relationship is supposed always to be one of *hlobonga* only.

A wife is not allowed any frivolous liberties, not even a mild flirtation except at the risk of serious trouble from her husband and at least a beating. But they say, 'some wives still take a chance!'

A polygamous household or kraal is a well-organised establishment based on old traditional customs and laws which have stood the tests of time. They are laws of precedence, etiquette and of discipline which make the system work probably far better than an outsider would consider feasible.

A system of a seniority rating among the wives is one of the major factors which keeps the mechanism intact. Each wife has her own place in the structure and she is well aware of what her privileges and obligations are. Above all the lone husband's authority over them all constitutes a strong stabilising factor. In the husband's hands lies the master key, for it is by his strength of character and by his ability to control his women that grace or grudge rules in the home.

The principles and rules governing a many-wived kraal are legion and range from procedures like the placing of huts, to the husband's finesse in the attention he gives each wife. They are all important.

In order to outline some of the basic customs related to the organisation of such a kraal, it is perhaps best to begin at the beginning and consider the man who takes his first wife and with his father's permission sets up a new home of his own away from the paternal establishment.*

Unless there has been some irreconcilable rift between him and his father, the man will retain his clan name and the identification of his father's family, but if there has been a bad quarrel he may isolate himself from his parent and adopt his own or another name by which the people of his kraal will become known. If he is strong enough to stand as a good family head and a leader, his family unit may ultimately grow into a new sib and in years to come into an entirely new clan. This is how many clans have had their beginnings. We are more concerned here with the development and growth of the individual home or kraal of a many-wived man and with his wives, their status and with his love affairs.

To return to the man who starts his own establishment. The first thing he

*It will be recalled that, traditionally, sons join their father's kraal on marriage.

does is to select a site for his kraal. Ideally he chooses high ground with an outlook on all sides so that from it he has a view of any approaching enemies. This custom is a legacy from the days of the old Zulu warriors. He builds his 'great hut' or *ndlunkulu*, with its doorway facing eastwards to get the morning sun and with a forward slope away in front. Then he erects his cattle byre with a circular pole-fence immediately in front of his door separated by only a few metres from it. The main gateway to the byre by which the cattle enter is placed at the furthest point from the hut doorway which is in the same position in its circle as the entrance to the hut is, but it may have small subsidiary entrances at the back near the hut itself. If the man is ambitious and energetic he will, in due course, build a circular outer stockade using rough poles dug into the ground side by side to enclose the whole area. This includes not only the byre and his main hut, but also any new huts which may be built to cater for an enlarged family. It too has its main gateway or *sango* in the same position in this outer circle as those of the main hut and the cattle byre, so that cattle on entering go straight through it into the byre. Traditionally this outer stockade is for protection from enemies but many kraals today no longer build them. Between the outer stockade and the byre fence runs a wide passageway along which all new huts are built with their backs to the outer stockade and their doors opening on to the passageway so that they look on to the byre fence. The passageway is used by the occupants of the kraal and any guests who visit them in all their comings and goings.

As a visitor approaches the establishment from the outside and stops to look in through the gateway or *sango* of the main stockade, he sees the passageway stretching away to the right and to the left of him and directly in front of him is the entrance to the byre. From this position of looking in from the kraal entrance, the half of the establishment on his right is literally known as the Right-Hand Side and that on his left as the Left-Hand Side. This is an important delineation of the establishment and a vital division of the kraal because by it the status of the wives in a polygamous marriage – and of their children – is decided. Those of the Right-Hand Side constitute the main house and those of the Left-Hand Side the supporting house. The *right* side carries the weight and the power and provides the future heir to lead the family.

A chief's main wife, or *nkosikazi*, is chosen in consultation with his clan who provide the *lobolo* cattle for her and this marriage invariably takes place after the chief already has several wives. She is therefore likely to be younger than any of his first wives and she provides the heir for the chief. Basically the idea of this late marriage is that such a son will be too young to become a threat to his father's seat during the old man's lifetime.

The *first* wife of a commoner as opposed to that of the chief, is his main wife or *nkosikazi* and she, with him, shares the main hut or *ndlunkulu* at the top of the perimeter which overlooks the kraal grounds. This main hut in a kraal is always bigger than any other which may subsequently be built for additional wives or for the man's children and it is the 'Great House' of the man and his *nkosikazi*. When the *nkosikazi* becomes pregnant, her husband builds her a hut first in line on the right-hand side and a little ahead of his own hut. As he emerges from his door the new hut is therefore immediately on his left, but it is also the first of the official right-hand side huts which, as has been explained, is taken from the right-hand side of the kraal as one enters the main gateway of the establishment from the *outside*.

The chief wife lives in her new hut for her pregnancy and for a period after that while her child is small, but even when she returns to the 'Great House' she retains the other as her private residence. She is not only her husband's 'chief wife', but – if he goes polygamous later – the head of the right-hand side of his kraal. Her son will be the future head of the family and his father's heir. The second wife the man takes is assistant to the *nkosikazi* but head of the left-hand side, or supporting house. Her hut is built on the opposite side to that of the *nkosikazi* and so is in the same position on the left. As the establishment grows with more wives and their children, so the huts go progressively forward in the two arms of a circle towards the main gateway to *sango* of the kraal. Ideally this constitutes the perfect layout of an orthodox kraal, but in actual practice the contours and the lay of the land on which a man builds seldom lend themselves to the construction of such an establishment.

A third wife, instead of being third in the wives' seniority is again a right-hand wife and joins the *nkosikazi* with a new hut placed forward of hers on the right-hand side, so that she is second in seniority by virtue of belonging to the main house. If the chief wife or *nkozikazi* bears no son, then the first son of the next senior right-hand wife in line will be the heir. It can happen that no sons at all are born to the main house, but provision is made for this eventuality in that a father may then take a son from a left-hand mother and give him to the senior right-hand wife to adopt and bring up as her own child and as his heir.

The Zulu say that the child's mother does not object to this arrangement because it is 'the way of the Zulu', and it is the family head's wish and it is necessary. It is also an honour for her son to be so chosen.

If by any chance the barren chief wife or another right-hand wife should subsequently produce a son of her own, then the head can replace the adopted son as heir. To compensate him the adopted son is then moved out of his father's home when he is old enough and given an independent establishment of his own in a separate area to avoid any future conflict between the two boys. The boy who moves out retains his father's family name and clan just as if he had stayed at home.

Another interesting situation develops when or if the right-hand wife or wives dies prematurely because a polygamous kraal may not be without a main house. In this case, instead of looking for a further *new* wife, the husband may promote a left-hand wife to the main house. He usually chooses the youngest of them and promotes her over the others to the position of *nkosikazi*. He chooses her, in particular, because as junior she has no status anyway, whereas the older wives of the left do have their respective seniorities and responsibilities related to their positions in the supporting house.

In effect the status of wives alternates between right-hand side and left-hand side according to their order of marriage, which means that the odd numbers of one, three and five are always right-hand and the even numbers are of the left-hand or supporting house. In describing the significance of his two 'houses' a Zulu man has the habit of clenching his right fist and flexing his muscles of that arm and saying, '*this* is the right. The side with *power!*' As already indicated, the eldest son of the *nkosikazi* is heir to his father's entire estate and is the future leader of his family line. Sons of the left-hand side have few or no claims unless their father specifically wishes any of them to inherit any of his possessions.

A question I am frequently asked about multiple wives is whether they are

THE FULLNESS OF TIME

A fashion in dress in the deep south of Natal near the Umtamvuna River. The girl's half-dyed hair, treated with clay and fat, signifies that she is eligible for courtship and marriage.

177

An engaged girl of the Ntombela clan in the mid-North. Her leg-bands are 'fixtures' made from soft wire painstakingly wound around horsetail hair (if available) – which is tough and resilient – or failing that, the next best substitute. She has a wig of knitting wool around her face but her head-dress is natural hair interwoven with knitting wool and packed inside with aromatic herbs.

Girls dressed in young men's outfits to 'court for their brother'. When a young man is unsuccessful in winning a girl's affection he sometimes asks his sisters to go and court for him. The girls here are dressed for this purpose . . .

One of the girls way-lays the
sought-after girl by the roadside and . . .

. . . when she comes along with a
friend on the way to fetch water, the
two girls with a mission accost her
and sing the praises of their forlorn
brother 'who is pining away for the
want of her love' .

In the three-day wedding ceremony a bride spends much of her time in the background. She sits quietly in a specific hut with her bridesmaids. The fringe over her eyes is part of the payment of respect (hlonipha) practice. The custom is primarily based on the need for a young wife to show respect to her husband and to her father-in-law.

Left: Many Zulu people are natural actors and love an audience. The young man here demonstrated to me part of the wedding ceremony and showed how the bridegroom, now no longer a timid and restrained suitor, should assert his manly authority on his marriage and give his bride a lecture on her new role.

A photograph taken at the southern end of the spectacular Valley of a Thousand Hills. A particular interest in it is the beadwork which differs substantially in colours and in style from that seen in most other parts.

185

The young man here lectures on how he
likes his maize stamped – an act especially
performed for my benefit. The little girl
appears to be giving the matter some thought.

A pregnant woman wearing a maternity
apron of wild antelope skin. The apron is
to make the child fleet of foot and agile like
the buck and full of grace and good health.

A married couple who have served their family well.

When a man reaches old age, he finds the skull of an ox and places it in the trunk of a tree outside his hut. 'This . . .' he says, 'is my evidence to all who pass this way that I have done my duty in life.'

A man in his advanced years regards it as his pleasure and privilege to watch the world at work.

Then comes the grave and to mark his resting place – especially in the case of a chief – his people plant a tree over the spot.

The Zulu say that sometimes a spirit becomes upset by the behaviour of his family back home and so goes down to the bottom of the sea to contemplate . . . and that is why, the Zulu say, when you come back from a visit to the sea and you bring your friend a bottle of sea water always put in a little sand . . . otherwise you may leave the spirit behind alone forever.

jealous and if they fight amongst themselves. My personal opinion on this is that the women would hardly be human if they did not disagree sometimes. But the rural tribespeople have lived with this system a long, long time and the women have accepted sharing a husband as normal. Furthermore, many of the wives seem proud to have been selected by a man who might already have a few attractive wives and still want *them,* and is willing to give many cattle for them.

In regard to the question of quarrelling, one man who has chief's blood in his veins, summed up the situation beautifully for me. He said: 'Sometimes they don't fight much and if they do, their husband gives them a good beating and that stops them. But, he added 'I've got four and they fight like the thunder roaring!' He paused and looked into the hills about him. 'So I split them up and gave each one their own home and their own cows for milk and their own piece of ground to plant their maize and now they live on those far hills over there, each with their own hill'.

In a polygamous kraal, the 'Great House' or *ndlunkulu* is, as I have said, the lord and master's 'official' hut which he shares with his *nkosikazi.* He should not monopolise her or any other of his wives and so must endeavour to distribute his time more or less equally between them. From four days up to a week at a time with each of them at her hut is considered a fair sort of basis, but despite the consequences of probable quarrels it is said that husbands inevitably end up favouring one wife more than another.

Between visits to individual wives and sometimes to his sweetheart, the husband retires to a small, private hut of his own which he keeps so that he may relax there in privacy. The Zulu call this his 'house to cool off in' or *ndlu yoku phola.*

When the time comes for him to visit any particular wife he does not simply arrive unannounced. That would be poor etiquette. Instead, he formally advises her of his coming by sending her a message through one of his small sons by his great wife, to say: 'Bring on water. I wish to bath.' She understands what he means. In the evening he arrives and as he enters takes his place on the right hand side of the hut. This is the place of the man of the house and she stays on her left-hand side while they sit and chat. If it is cold there will be a fire in the house on the floor between them.

Ultimately, when time for bed comes, she brings on the bath water in the curved surface of a broken clay pot or *dengezi* and they both wash themselves. This, the Zulu have told me, is customary before sex between a Zulu man and his wife. Then he goes to his sleeping mat on his side of the hut. If he wishes to have her company he calls her over to join him. She may not of her own account initiate this advance, because it is his prerogative and she may not go to his side unless he invites her. At his suggestion she crosses the floor, dressed just in a small loin cloth, to be with him.

> *Outside, in the cattle byre*
> *The cows low and their calves answer*
> *Yet, the man and his wife hear nothing of it all*
> *Because, beside them in the hearth*
> *The fire's last embers*
> *Busily send up little flames*
> *To paint strange dancing figures on the wall*
> *In soft grey shadows and garments tinged in gold.*

Layout of an Orthodox Polygamous Zulu Kraal

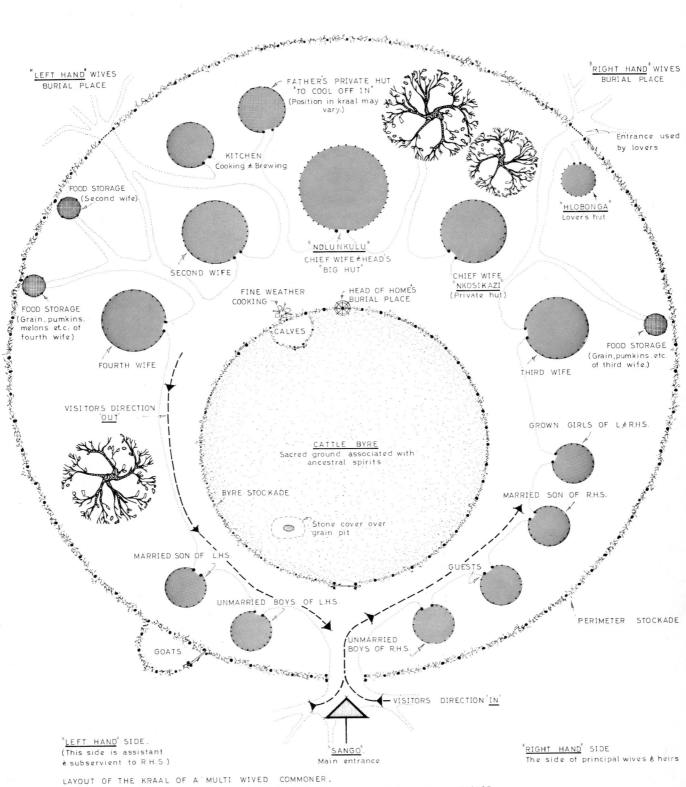

"LEFT HAND" WIVES
BURIAL PLACE

FATHER'S PRIVATE HUT
"TO COOL OFF IN"
(Position in kraal may
vary.)

"RIGHT HAND" WIVES
BURIAL PLACE

Entrance used
by lovers

KITCHEN
Cooking & Brewing

FOOD STORAGE
(Second wife)

"HLOBONGA"
Lovers hut

"NDLUNKULU"
CHIEF WIFE & HEAD'S
"BIG HUT"

SECOND WIFE

CHIEF WIFE
"NKOSIKAZI"
(Private hut)

FOOD STORAGE
(Grain, pumkins,
melons etc. of
fourth wife)

FINE WEATHER
COOKING

HEAD OF HOME'S
BURIAL PLACE

FOOD STORAGE
(Grain, pumkins. etc.
of third wife.)

CALVES

FOURTH WIFE

THIRD WIFE

VISITORS DIRECTION
'OUT'

GROWN GIRLS OF L.& R.H.S.

CATTLE BYRE
Sacred ground associated with
ancestral spirits

MARRIED SON OF R.H.S.

BYRE STOCKADE

Stone cover over
grain pit

MARRIED SON OF L.H.S.

GUESTS

UNMARRIED BOYS OF L.H.S.

PERIMETER STOCKADE

GOATS

UNMARRIED
BOYS OF R.H.S.

VISITORS DIRECTION 'IN'

"LEFT HAND" SIDE.
(This side is assistant
& subservient to R.H.S.)

"SANGO".
Main entrance

"RIGHT HAND" SIDE
The side of principal wives & heirs

LAYOUT OF THE KRAAL OF A MULTI WIVED COMMONER.
IN THE CASE OF A CHIEF THE MAIN WIFE IS NOT THE FIRST WIFE TAKEN IN MARRIAGE

Royal Dynasty of the Zulu

Details of Chiefs prior to Shaka were brought down orally, largely by court praise-singers and are based in the main on the deductions of Dr. A. T. Bryant – historian and anthropologist.

LUZUMANE
Legend places him as the first name in its memory; none know from whence he came or what his background was but tradition alleges he was father of

MALANDELA
±b1597–d1691. Nomad until he settled at last with wife Nozinja at Mandawe Hill near present Eshowe; two known sons, Qwabe and Zulu; on father's death Qwabe departed to form own clan and mother was protected by younger son

ZULU
±b1627–d1709. Grew in stature; gave his name to the family line and became founder of the famous Zulu *clan*; legend hazy on specific relationship of successor but generally accepts he was eldest son

PUNGA
±b1657–d1727. Died without male heir; allegedly succeeded by brother

MAGEBA
±b1660–d1745. According to tradition, inherited brother Punga's widow with chieftaincy; through her 'raised seed' for brother and fathered son named

NDABA
Reign ∓1745-1763
±b1697–d1763. His eldest son Xoko branched off to form own Gazini clan; Ndaba succeeded by younger son

JAMA
Reign ∓1763-1781
±b1727–d1781. Who ultimately left as heir only a *minor* son

SENZANGAKONA
Reign (1781)
1783-1816
±b1757–d1816. His eldest sister Mkabayi and various uncles acted as regents in his minority until 1783; in 33 years reign his numerous wives gave him many children amongst whom were the famous Shaka, Dingane, Mpande, Mhlangana and Sigujana, his nominated heir.

SIGUJANA
Reign short-lived in 1816
b1790–d1816. Assumed leadership on Senzangakona's death; promptly murdered by Ngwadi at Shaka's behest; succeeded by

SHAKA
Reign 1816-1828
b1787–d1828. Son of Senzangakona and Nandi conceived out of wedlock; Nandi subsequently taken as third wife but exiled together with Shaka when he was six; Shaka experienced unhappy childhood until befriended by powerful Mtetwa king Dingiswayo who launched him on a military career and helped him take the Zulu clan leadership from Sigujana; embarked on training own warriors with ideas of expansion by conquest; after Dingiswayo's death assumed leadership of Mtetwa; tales of his wars against major opposition – King Zwide of the Ndwandwe – are told in many epics and his ultimate complete victory left Shaka supreme leader of a new nation – the Zulu Nation; in his reign, the first white settlers came to Natal in 1824; at his death he commanded 50 000 warriors; assasinated and succeeded by half-brother

DINGANE
Reign 1828-1840

b1785– d1840. Another son of Senzangakona; aided and abetted by aged aunt Mkabayi, plotted Shaka's death; assisted by half-brother Mhlangana and head of household guards Mbopa, he assasinated Shaka then deceitfully murdered both his accomplices; took Zulu throne in 1828; bloodthirsty, cruel, 12-year reign; early 1838 murdered Piet Retief and 66 Boer followers; 16th December 1838 defeated by Boers at Blood River; half-brother Mpande with his following deserted Dingane and crossed Tugela; found refuge with Boers whom he joined to conquer Dingane finally in 1840; Dingane fled to Swaziland; murdered by unknown assasins; succeeded by half-brother

MPANDE
Reign 1840-1872

b1790– d1872. Son of Senzangakona; originally spared death in time of Dingane's early purge as king because considered weak and simple; thirty-two years reign largely prosperous and peaceful; Zulu turned to pastoral activities rather than warring; last years of reign disturbed by rivalry between two sons; Cetshwayo and Mbuyazi contending for heirship; violent battle terminated the struggle; Cetshwayo's followers, who became known as the Usutu, annihilated Mbuyazi and a following of 23 000 people on the Banks of the Tugela where the John Ross Bridge now crosses it; apart from Mbuyazi, Cetshwayo's Usutu warriors killed five other sons of Mpande and, it is said, one of Dingane's named Shepstone; Mpande died at 82 succeeded by

CETSHWAYO
Reign (Intermittent)
1872-1884

b1834– d1884. A natural leader, but unlike peace-loving father, a warrior; revived his *impis;* by this time British had colonised Natal; British lack of understanding of Zulu social customs, like polygamy, irksome as was their lack of appreciation of Zulu traditions – contributory factors to war of 1879; January 1879 devastating defeat of British at Isandlwana; a few hours later at Rorke's Drift Zulu fought them in one of British military history's greatest episodes; Cetshwayo defeated 4th July 1879 at Ulundi; British arbitrarily divided Zululand into 13 artificial chieftaincies; Cetshwayo banished; Queen Victoria ineffectually restored his throne in 1883; died 1884 at young age of 50 at Eshowe; buried in fringe of Nkandla forest; eldest son and legitimate heir as leader of Zulu peoples, was

DINIZULU
Reign (Shadow
Throne)
1884-1888
1898-1907

b1868– d1913. Aged 16 at time of succession; power struggle between his royal Usutu clan (founded by Cetshwayo) and Chief Sibebu with his Mandhlakazi; Boers of Natal supported Dinizulu and British Sibebu; also territorial struggle between Boer, British and Zulu; 1884 at 16 Dinizulu proclaimed king of Zulu by Republican Boers; not recognised by British; turbulent, disrupted 29 years followed; in 1887 caught in crossfire of triangular struggle for territory; 1888 banished to St. Helena by British for activities against the Crown of England; 1897 control of Zululand given to British colony of Natal; 1898 Dinizulu returned and reinstated as head of Usutu faction with limited authority; 1907 imprisoned for complicity in Bambatha rebellion arising out of Natal's harsh taxation; released 1910 by General Louis Botha after incorporation of Natal and Zululand into new Union of South Africa but remained in exile in district of Middelburg Transvaal until death in 1913; buried in Zululand; Dinizulu's son Solomon Nkayishana Maphumzana proclaimed heir by Dinizulu – became known as

SOLOMON
Reign (1913)
1916-1933

b1880– d1933. Assumed chieftaincy of Usutu on father's death; recognised as such by S.A. Government in 1916; as leader of Royal Usutu was hereditary head of Zulu people; recognised as Paramount Chief of Zulu in 1919 by S.A. Government; had 40 known wives including one Christian; on death in 1933 succeeded by chief wife Ntombeni's son

CYPRIAN
Reign (1933)
1948-1968

b1924– d1968. Aged 9; 1933 – 1948 Prince Mshiyeni KaDinizulu acted as Regent; in 1948 a 20 year reign began; many constitutional changes in life of Zulu nation; 1953 S.A. Government made known concept of homeland status; 1970 first Territorial Authority for Zulu people established and Zulu homeland defined; 30.3.1972 first Legislative Assembly of KwaZulu constituted by S.A. Parliamentary Proclamation and Chief Gatsha Buthelezi – cousin of King Cyprian on maternal side – nominated Chief Executive; town of Nongoma temporarily consolidated as capital pending completion of structures at Ulundi – Cetshwayo's old royal kraal; King Cyprian died 1968 succeeded by son and heir

ZWELITHINI
GOODWILL
Reign (1968)
1971-

b1948– Aged 20; 1968-1971 Prince Israel Mcwayizeni KaSolomon acted as Regent; 3rd December 1971, Goodwill installed by S.A. Government at Khethomthandayo near Nongoma as Paramount Chief of the Zulu Nation consisting of in excess of 280 clans; tribal repetition of ceremony followed at the King's Royal Household on following day 4th December 1971.

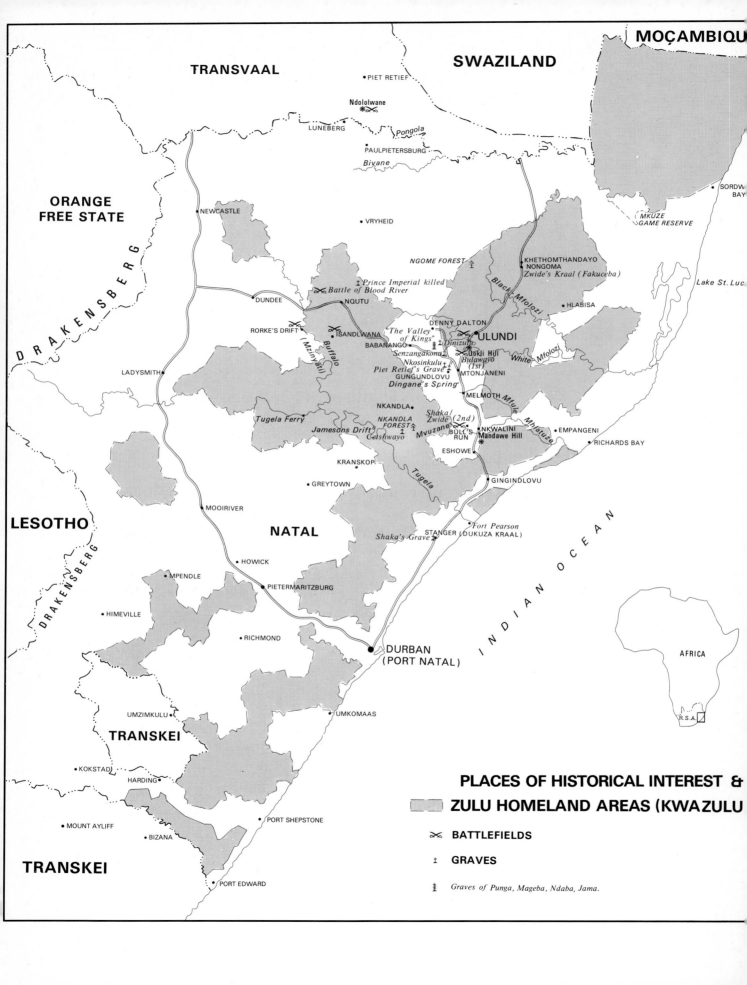

MOÇAMBIQU

TRANSVAAL

SWAZILAND

• PIET RETIEF

Ndololwane

LUNEBERG

Pongola

PAULPIETERSBURG

Bivane

ORANGE
FREE STATE

• NEWCASTLE

• VRYHEID

SORDW
BAY

*MKUZE
GAME RESERVE*

Lake St.Luc.

D R A K E N S B E R G

NGOME FOREST

KHETHOMTHANDAYO
NONGOMA
Zwide's Kraal (Fakuceba)

Black Mfolozi

‡ *Prince Imperial killed*
⚔ *Battle of Blood River*

• DUNDEE

• HLABISA

RORKE'S DRIFT

• NQUTU

DENNY DALTON

ISANDLWANA

*"The Valley
of Kings"*

‡ *Dinizulu*

ULUNDI

Qokli Hill

LADYSMITH •

(Mzinyati)

Buffalo

BABANANGO
Senzangakona‡
Nkosinkulu‡
Piet Retief's Grave‡
GUNGUNDLOVU
Dingane's Spring

*Bulawayo
(1st)*
MTONJANENI

White Mfolozi

MELMOTH

Mfule

NKANDLA

*Shaka/
Zwide (2nd)*

Mhlatuze

Tugela Ferry

NKANDLA
FOREST‡

Mvuzane

BULL'S
RUN

NKWALINI
Mandawe Hill

• EMPANGENI

Jamesons Drift

Cetshwayo‡

• RICHARDS BAY

• KRANSKOP

ESHOWE

Tugela

• GREYTOWN

GINGINDLOVU

• MOOIRIVER

NATAL

Fort Pearson
STANGER (DUKUZA KRAAL)

Shaka's Grave

I N D I A N   O C E A N

LESOTHO

• MPENDLE

• HOWICK

• RICHMOND

PIETERMARITZBURG

• HIMEVILLE

D R A K E N S B E R G

AFRICA

UMZIMKULU •

• UMKOMAAS

R.S.A.

TRANSKEI

DURBAN
(PORT NATAL)

• KOKSTAD

HARDING

PLACES OF HISTORICAL INTEREST &

• MOUNT AYLIFF

• BIZANA

• PORT SHEPSTONE

ZULU HOMELAND AREAS (KWAZULU

TRANSKEI

⚔ **BATTLEFIELDS**

• PORT EDWARD

‡ **GRAVES**

‡ *Graves of Punga, Mageba, Ndaba, Jama.*

Bibliography

BECKER, Peter. *Trails and Tribes in Southern Africa*, Hart Davis, MacGibbon, London, 1975.

BINNS, C. T. *Dinuzulu*, Longmans Green & Co., London, South Africa, 1968.
The Last Zulu King, Longmans Green & Co., London, 1963.
The Warrior People, Howard Timmins, Cape Town, 1974.

BRYANT, A. T. *The Zulu People*, Shuter and Shooter, Pietermaritzburg, 1949, Second Edition 1967.
Olden Times in Zululand and Natal, Longmans Green & Co., London, New York, 1929.
Zulu-English Dictionary, Juta & Co., Cape Town, 1905.

BULPIN, T. V. *Natal and the Zulu Country*, Books of Africa (Pty.) Ltd., Cape Town, 1966.

DOKE, C. M., MALCOLM, D. McK., SIKAKANA, J. M. A. (compiled by). *English-Zulu Dictionary*, Witwatersrand University Press, Johannesburg, 1958.

ELLIOTT, Aubrey. *The Magic World of the Xhosa*, Collins, London, 1970.

FYNN, Henry Francis. *The Diary of Henry Francis Fynn* (compiled from original sources and edited by Stuart, James & Malcolm D. McK.), Shuter & Shooter, Pietermaritzburg, 1969.

HAMMOND-TOOKE, W. D. (edited by). *The Bantu-Speaking Peoples of Southern Africa*, Routledge & Kegan Paul, London/Boston, second edition 1974.

HOLDEN, William C. *History of the Colony of Natal*, Struik Publishers, Cape Town, 1963.

ISAACS, Nathanial. *Travels and Adventure in Eastern Africa* (Natal), C. Struik, Cape Town, 1970. Newly revised and edited in one volume, with a biography by the Author.
Notes and Appendices by Herman, Louis & Kirby, Percival R.

KRIGE, Eileen Jensen. *The Social System of the Zulus*, Longmans Green & Co., London, 1936; 2nd edition Shuter & Shooter, Pietermaritzburg, 1950.

LUGG, H. C. *Historic Natal & Zululand*, Shuter & Shooter, Pietermaritzburg, S.A., 1949.

MORRIS, Donald R. *The Washing of the Spears*, Jonathan Cape, London, 1966.

RITTER, E. A. *Shaka Zulu*, Longmans Green & Co., Ltd., London, 1955.

SAMUELSON, R. C. *Long, Long Ago*, Knox Printing & Publishing Co., Durban, 1929.

SMAIL, J. L. *With Shield and Assegai*, Howard Timmins, Cape Town, 1969.

Glossary of Zulu Words

The words listed below are root words without prefixes except where specifically considered necessary because of usage, in which case prefixes are in brackets.

(ama)Bele	In this case sorghum grain used in Zulu beer-making. In the spoken language today *amabele* appears to have become the standard word
(ama)Dlozi	pl. Ancestral spirits
(ama)Dumbe	Edible tubers of the arum family grown by the Zulu. In the spoken language today *amadumbe* appears to have become the standard word
(ama)Si	Sour or curdled milk – staple diet of Zulu. In the spoken language today *amasi* appears to have become the standard word
(ama)Zulu	pl. Zulu people. Lit. 'The People of the Sky' or 'Sons of Zulu'
Angoma	See *sangoma*
Awu	Expression of surprise, now perhaps used less than '*Hawu*'
Baba	'Sir!' A respectful form of address for an honoured or superior man. See also *sakubona, sanibona, sawubona*
Bayede	The royal greeting, greeting or salute for the Zulu king
Bongo	see *sibongo*
Buzi	see *mbuzi*
Cece	Lovers dance, engagement dance, the dance to celebrate a girl's coming of marriageable age
Dengele	Old clay pot with chipped edges
Dengezi	Potsherd. Curved portion of a broken clay pot in which diviners and medicine-men burn incense and medicines. Also used as a washing utensil
Dlelo	Dish or container
Dlozi	Ancestral spirit see *amadlozi*
Dumbe	See *amadumbe*
Dwaba	See *sidwaba*
Emula	To re-commence partaking of sour milk, *amasi*, after a period of abstention from it because of a taboo. Same as *omula*
Gonqo	A portion of a hut partitioned off with a reed mat to isolate a female during the observance of certain rituals
Hamba	Go, proceed, walk
Hamba kahle	'Go well' 'Farewell'
Hawu	An emphatic expression of surprise. Perhaps more commonly used now than the milder *awu*
Hlobonga	A form of external intercourse practised by unmarried couples
Hlonipha	To pay respect – to a person or ancestral spirit – in ritualistic ways
Hluzo	Beer strainer woven from grass or other suitable material

(i)Cece	See *cece*
(i)Mpi	Regiment or army of Zulu warriors
(i)Nyanga	see *nyanga*
(isi)Bongo	See *sibongo*
(isi)Cuthe	One with unpierced, and so 'unopened' ears. Often used derisively in respect of someone who has not followed the tribal custom
(isi)Dwaba	see *sidwaba*
Jabula	Rejoice
Ka-	Prefix meaning 'of' e.g. in the sense 'child *of*'
Kahle	Well e.g. 'Hamba kahle' – 'go well'
Khamba	Clay beer pot
Kwa-	Adverb meaning 'at the place of' (so and so)
KwaZulu	'The place of the Zulu'. Zulu homeland
Kwemula	see *emula*
Lala	sleep
Lobola	v. The act of delivery of *lobolo* – see *lobolo*
Lobolo	n. The cattle or other value delivered to a bride's father for his daughter by her future husband
Madala	Friendly form of address for an old man
Mame	Mother. Also used as respectful form of address to a senior married woman
Maphoyisa	See *phoyisa*
Mbuzi	Goat
Mpi	See *impi*
Msamo	Storage area at back of hut. In the family head's hut the *msamo* is visited or frequented by his ancestral spirits. It is a 'place of the spirits' although not the only one
Muthi	Medicine
Mvelinqangi	'The one who came first', Creator and source of all things – usually known also as Nkulunkulu
Mvula	Rain
Mvulankulu	Big rain
Ndlovu	Lit. 'elephant' but also used by the Zulu as title or praise name for their king
Ndlunkulu	The 'big house', the hut of a family head or chief
Ndlu yokuphola	Married man's private hut, 'his hut to cool off in'
Ngiyabonga	I praise you, 'thank you'
Ngonyama	Lit. lion, but also used by the Zulu as title or praise name for their king
Ngozi	Accident
Ni	(interrogation) what, where e.g. in where is it?
Nkomo	Head of cattle
Nkosinkulu	'Great Chief' and early Zulu progenitor – doubt exists as to just *who* he was
Nkosikazi	A chief's or polygamous man's principal wife, in modern times also used as a respectful form of address for any married woman
Nkulunkulu	'The Greatest of the Great', the Founder of all, The Supreme Being – see also Mvelinqangi
Nkunzana	An indigenous plant with a formidable three-pronged thorn which the Zulu call an *nkunzana*. In English they are often referred to as 'devil thorns'

No-	Prefix to a female's name whether she is unmarried or married
Nozingozi	Name meaning 'Miss/Mrs Accident'
Numzana	Head of kraal, headman, polite form of address
Nyamakazi	(Borrowed from Xhosa) wild animal
Nyanga	Healer, doctor, herbalist
Omula	see *emula*
Phini	Lit. stirring stick, but used figuratively for 'handmaiden'
Phoko	Type of millet used by Zulu for beer-making
Phoyisa	Policeman
Sakubona	Form of greeting, good-day (see *sawubona*)
Samo	see *msamo*
Sango	Main entrance or gateway of a kraal
Sangoma	Diviner, witch-doctor. In the spoken language today *sangoma* appears to have become the standard word
Sanibona	Lit. 'We see you' reciprocal greeting
Sawubona	Lit. I see you, greeting to some extent superceding *sakubona*
Si	see *amasi*
Sibongo	Clan name. In the spoken language today *sibongo* appears to have become the standard word
Sidwaba	A married woman's or engaged girl's leather skirt. In the spoken language today *sidwaba* appears to have become the standard word
Siyabonga	'We thank you, we praise you'
Sondela	Come here, come closer
Thakathi	Witch or wizard, evil one working with magic or supernatural media
Thi	see *muthi*
Thomba	Advent of puberty
Thombo	Malt for brewing beer
Tshwala	Beer
Ukuthelelana amanzi	(Phrase) Lit. 'pouring water for each other' relates to a peace making ceremony between two men
(u)Msamo	see *msamo*
(u)Muthi	see *muthi*
Wena	You
Yoh	Exclamation of surprise
Zulu	Lit. Sky or space above. Those of the Zulu clan or tribe

Index of Subject Matter

Index of Photographic Chapters